A PARENT'S GUIDE TO RAISING A RACE DRIVER

ENZO MUCCI

ISBN: 9781916219021

THANK YOU EVERYONE

I want to thank every driver, ever parent, every team manager, every driver manager, every driver coach and pretty much everyone else who I have worked with over the years. The lessons that I have learned from all of you have helped me create another book that will help people achieve their goals in racing.

As for you, the parent, I would also like to thank you for caring so much about your child's racing career. I hope they understand how lucky they are to have someone like you supporting them as they strive to make a career in motorsport.

If it wasn't for all the people that I have just mentioned on this page, this book wouldn't have been possible to create.

Thank you all.

CONTENTS

DEAR PARENT

Before we dive into this I want to give you a warm welcome and give you a heads up for what you are about to read.

My name is Enzo Mucci and since the Nineties I've been fortunate enough to work with race drivers as they pursue their racing dreams. I work as their performance coach, which means that I teach them the mental and motorsport-specific skills that help them perform better on and off track.

This role has enabled me to understand what skills a race driver needs in order for them to succeed. And, more importantly for this book, it has given me an insight into the dynamics between drivers and their parents. Over time I have had the opportunity to witness what seems to work and what doesn't in this area.

Unfortunately there isn't much education or information out there that teaches us how motorsport operates, so many people enter this sport completely blind. The industry will often take advantage of people in this situation, leading drivers and parents to make costly mistakes which can prematurely end a driver's career, and also put some serious pressure on family relationships.

That's why I'm here writing this. I want to help parents like you navigate this complex and expensive sport. My mission with this book is to give you information that you can take with you on your racing journey and provide some clarity in the sometimes-bizarre world of motorsport.

I really look forward to sharing this information with you.

Enzo

HOW THIS BOOK WORKS

Let's start off by explaining what we're going to do here and how this book is laid out so you can make the most of it.

I have designed this book so it can be used as a trouble-shooting guide (just like the booklet that comes with a new TV or piece of furniture). Each chapter covers the most common challenges that parents face and within each chapter I will give you my best advice on that particular topic.

Some of these topics are so broad, I could write a book on each one... but to save your time and help you take immediate action, I will cut to the chase in every chapter and offer you quick solutions so we can make this as effective as possible. In short, there will be no fluff and not too much in the way of storytelling here.

If you prefer, you can use this book like you would an instruction manual. Once you have read through Part 1 to understand the philosophy of the book, you can jump to the chapters that are most relevant for you to get some immediate ideas for how to overcome those specific challenges.

I've split this book into three parts:

Part 1 - Alignment

I encourage you to read all the chapters in this first part so you can align with what I'm teaching and understand the important aspects of being a race driver's parent.

Part 2 - Mental Performance Training

Here we will focus on aspects that are related to your driver's mental skills. All the training strategies taught in this section of the book have been tried and tested, they have all worked on drivers competing in all levels of motorsport.

Part 3 - Career Advice

In the final part we will cover the common career-related challenges that parents and drivers face and I will offer some advice for how to deal with these challenges.

The term "Your Driver"

Even though you are reading this to help your child as they tackle the world of motorsport, I will often refer to your child as 'Your Driver'. I will do this due to the different age ranges of parents that will read this book. I felt that using the term 'Your Driver' would be easier linguistically and easier for you to read.

The information here

I want to make it clear that the information I provide in this book is simply advice, and you should be the person who decides whether the advice is relevant or not to your particular situation.

I will put many suggestions and strategies to you but ultimately you are to judge what's worth taking on.

OK that's it for the intro part done, let's begin...

PART 1:
ALIGNMENT

CHAPTER 1
THE ROLE OF A PARENT

As you will have found, there are plenty of good and bad things about motorsport. But one thing that really grinds my gears is how the industry often leaves parents in the dark, with little to no advice on how they should support their child's racing career.

Being a parent in motorsport is no walk in the park. You are expected to be a jack-of-all-trades, from being a cheerleader to a bankroller to a shoulder to cry on. You are also required to do this while navigating the murky waters of the racing world. This is not easy.

Credit where credit's due

In the world of sport, we tend to focus on the athletes themselves and their mental fortitude, but we forget about the unsung heroes behind the scenes who play an integral role in shaping these champions.

While we acknowledge the impact that parents had on athletes such as Serena and Venus Williams, Tiger Woods, Floyd Mayweather, Joe Calzaghe and Michael Jordan, we rarely talk about the role of parents in the lives of race drivers – unless their parents were former race drivers themselves.

Despite this I firmly believe that parents are some of the most critical figures in motorsport. While we may hear about the extraordinary lengths that Anthony Hamilton and John Button went to for their sons' racing careers, the industry often overlooks the significance of parental involvement. Instead motorsport often treats the parents as if they are the people who are in some way a hindrance, but I beg to differ.

As someone who has been involved in the sport for some years now, I have seen first-hand the vital role parents play in the success of race drivers.

Parents like you demonstrate unwavering support and guidance, making sacrifices that often go unnoticed, but you are the backbone of your drivers' careers.

The reason I believe this is because as a parent you are the one who...

- Provides the support that your child needs
- Juggles their schooling schedule to enable them to race
- Wipes away their tears when things don't go to plan
- Puts the right people in place to help their career
- Stands on a corner in the rain as they turn laps
- Shares the car journey home after a tough race weekend
- Has the awkward conversations with race teams

Parents have given birth to – and nurtured the passion of – every driver on our grids. Without you, this sport simply wouldn't exist. You have not only provided your child with the resources needed, but also with the courage to go out there and compete.

As a coach I carry the emotional baggage that my drivers place upon me at each race weekend... but I get to go home afterwards so I can recharge myself ready for the next event. You, on the other hand, carry the weight of your child's performance on your shoulders 24/7.

The emotional rollercoaster that motorsport takes you on is one thing, but living with a young driver at home and dealing with the day-to-day repercussions of the last race weekend is non-stop for you.

That's one very important role that you are fulfilling and couple this with your unconditional love for your child or children, how can I not tip my hat to you?

I'm not saying this to blow smoke here, it's just a fact.

You are the significant other

The driver may be the person who is ultimately in control of their own work ethic and discipline, but the parent helps condition the mind of the driver on a daily basis.

This makes you one of the biggest influencers in your child's life.

You hold a significant amount of power in shaping the future of your child's personal and professional life. Your behaviour and words at home directly influence their mental model of the world, which ultimately shapes the path they take in life.

You have the ability to contribute to your child's Mental Matrix, which creates reality as they perceive it. It's a serious responsibility that shouldn't be taken lightly. As Uncle Ben in Spider-Man said: "With great power comes great responsibility" so as the first piece of advice in this book, I want you to understand just how crucial your role is in all of this.

I say that because it is easy for parents to feel left out and insignificant at times, especially when your child reaches an age where they don't show their love and appreciation like they used to.

Every parent has their own parenting style and it's all about finding the right balance, but if you can strike that balance well, then you will significantly help your child get the best out of themselves.

I want to commend your commitment to helping your child succeed (I can tell that you are committed because you are reading this book right now). I respect the challenge you have undertaken and I am here to give you everything I can to help your child reach their full potential.

Truth and perspective

Throughout this book I will be giving things to you straight – I really don't want to hold back here. But first, let's take a step back and gain a true perspective on the industry as a whole.

Part 1 of this book will enable you to take a step back, to give you the helicopter view, so we can see things for how they really are and help you approach things in the most effective way possible.

CHAPTER 2
THE GOOD, THE BAD & THE UGLY

Having made it this far in life, you will have already endured the inevitable challenges that life treats us to. You have navigated your way through the schooling system, you went on to earn a living, you survived arduous relationships, you created a career for yourself, you will have experienced some personal and professional highs and lows, and along the way you created a family of your own.

You already deserve a round of applause for getting this far.

However, the icing on the cake for you came when your little cherub of a son or a daughter uttered the magical words "I want to be a race driver" or "I want to go karting".

Alternatively, you introduced your young one to racing and what started off as a bit of fun on the weekends grew into something more serious.

Either way you have been thrust into a unique sport that doesn't come with any kind of user manual. Motorsport isn't the kind of pastime where you can go down the pub with your friends to exchange experiences and advice. It's not exactly mainstream...

This means that as a parent (the person who is supposed to have all the answers) you find yourself in a situation that is outside of your comfort zone. Yet you are still the one who has to balance things both time-wise and money-wise in order to make all this happen.

It lures you in

Motorsport can be viewed as a mistress that lures people in gently with its glamorous exterior but once it gets a hold of you and you become hooked, it then tests you and plays with your emotions. From time to time motorsport will give you some love as a reminder for why you fell for it in the first place, but in between these times you will endure long periods of pain.

Sounds like a lot of marriages we know, right?

Well, whether you stick with this relationship or not, you quickly learn that things are often not as they seemed in the beginning.

Navigating your way through a racing career is like navigating your way through a labyrinth. The treasure at the end urges you to continue, but the deeper you go into it the more chances you have of taking a wrong turn, falling into traps and even getting lost.

Hence why I want to give this global view of the world you are involved in.

The Good, the Bad & the Ugly

As you can tell (or may know from my online content) I often paint a bleak picture of racing because I like to give people reality checks. But from what you have experienced, you will know full well that it isn't all doom and gloom; it can actually be the most magnificent sport at times.

There are plenty of good things about motor racing and what it can offer you and your child.

I have called this chapter The Good, The Bad & The Ugly because I want to share with you the full picture of what your child is involved in.

The Good

The good thing about motorsport is that it provides its competitors (not just the drivers) with personal experiences that help them improve their mental, physical and business games.

It's the same for every other sport, due to the challenges that we face whilst competing, we inherit personal skills that help us tackle many other aspects and challenges in our lives. This is something that every parent wants for their child.

Motorsport really tests the participants because on top of the sporting side they also must address the financial and team aspects related to it. There are countless variables and moving parts that must all run in sync if a driver or a team are to win, which is an ideal environment for self-development.

Again, just like life itself.

A successful race driver shares quite a few similarities with a successful CEO because both of these 'job roles' require you to be a master at your craft whilst taking on the responsibility of running the whole show.

So if for some reason racing doesn't go to plan for a driver, then at least you know that your child or children will have learned some valuable life skills that will serve them well.

While in the racing world, if the driver fully applies themselves then they will learn:

- How to perform in a pressured environment

- How to lead a team
- How to overcome adversity
- How to consistently compete and perform at their best
- How to self-analyse and improve themselves
- How to make critical decisions
- How to learn from mistakes
- How to create their desired results
- How to deal with public failure and criticism
- How to multitask

For ease of reading, I will stop there because I could go on all day adding to this list. They even pick up skills that will help them in business – such as the art of persuasion, selling and public speaking.

All of this sounds great but I must stress that drivers only take on these skills if they are proactive and mentally 'on the offence' as they compete. They will miss out on these teachings if they get too much assistance from others because they will be protected from the hardship and the learning opportunities that this sport offers.

You often find that the drivers who are over-coached, do not pick up as many of these life skills compared to those who are more 'self-made'.

So as a quick lesson here, if you want your child to develop into a self-sufficient champion in racing and in life, always remember that they must be forced to put in the work themselves and personally take the metaphorical punches in the face. We will cover this topic more later.

It can improve your bond with them

On top of all these personal skills, we mustn't forget that racing can also bring a parent and child closer. At times it may feel as though it creates distance but if played correctly then you can use motorsport as a way to connect or reconnect with each other.

I know that your child may not show this and at times they will be downright rude to you, but believe me, they really do value you.

Racing can create an opportunity for you to spend more time with your child and to be on their team of people who will help them succeed. That is completely different from what most kids have with their parents, so I see this as a potential plus point when involved in motorsport.

There is obviously a very fine line between being supportive and being too overbearing – but if this balance is struck well then this sport can help create a special relationship between you.

It can be seen as a shared journey where you both stand shoulder-to-shoulder as you both take on the racing quest.

This may be hard to believe but once all this is done and dusted and you look back on the times that you and your child spent at the track, you will have plenty of memories stored up that will populate your mental scrapbook. I promise that you will refer to this period as 'The Good Times'.

It feeds your competitive spirit

Let's be honest here: when your child is racing it also feeds your own competitive spirit. This is something that we often lose as we are making an everyday living... but watching your child's name on the live timing, seeing them fighting on track and shooting for wins, is a great feeling.

It does this for me as a coach as well. My heart is pounding out of my chest when I am watching my drivers race, so I can only imagine what it does to you as a parent.

I've had parents who scream and shout as their child is racing – and on the flip side I have had other parents who can't even watch due to their own nerves – but all of them still love the feeling of competition and miss it when their child is no longer racing.

Personally I loved racing because it not only ticked all my emotional boxes but I also got to share it with my family. We used to go to the races in a small motorhome and camp out during our race weekends. These were good times and even though that was over 20 years ago, my parents still reminisce about that era.

Compare this to today: with my father living in Spain and my mother nearly four hours' drive away, I hardly see them. It's such a big difference compared to how we lived back then.

All in all, there are many great benefits that racing offers and I'm sure that you can think of more positives than I have mentioned here. Next, I want to turn our attention to the not-so-good aspects of being involved in this sport...

The Bad

This may be a sport that we all love; but as you know love resides right next door to hate, and there are plenty of so-called 'bad' things that come along with racing. People find it a little easier to list out the things they don't like about motorsport – and I am sure that some come to your mind right now – but let me give you some of the things that come to my mind.

The price

No surprise here... but motor racing is seriously expensive and due to the rise in the popularity of F1 (largely thanks to Netflix), at the time of writing we are seeing huge grids in the championships that lead up to motorsport's pinnacle.

This spike in popularity has driven prices up in the junior categories, to the point where we are now getting quotes from race teams in the region of €1 million euros per year to compete in F4.

This is bonkers but due to the drivers doing double campaigns, winter championships and stacks of testing, it is now the team's opportunity to cash in and have bidding wars.

This makes the entry level for the F1 ladder very difficult to achieve for drivers from working class or middle class backgrounds. There are still many drivers competing who are not from wealthy families, but they have to depend on rare opportunities if they are to advance.

For those who want to make it past the club racing level and progress towards GT or Touring Cars, they currently need about £150,000 per season to comfortably compete at the front in a worthwhile series. Even though this figure is more achievable, it is still a big ask to get that money together for a single season of racing.

Money has always been a serious hurdle for drivers, but in a world where sponsorship is needed, it is getting more difficult to sell due to companies having many more options when it comes to how to spend their marketing budget.

If you were to ask a company whether they prefer to spend £20,000 on sponsoring a race car to get new customers, or to spend that £20,000 on targeted social media marketing, I think you know which one would give them a better ROI.

Racing is expensive, and for me that is the number one bad thing about this sport. There is also no real structure or program in place that helps drivers compete without spending obscene amounts of money. It's about time this changed... somehow.

Disruption of their education

This may or may not be relevant to you but for some parents, education is seriously important. For obvious reasons many parents see the value in making sure their child has a degree or a good level of qualifications in a certain field.

However, if your child is racing then they are going to have to juggle their time between the circuit and the school. Racing takes up a lot of time so the schools that driver's go to must be very tolerant because they need to fit studying/schooling in whenever they can.

This is not an easy, so parents often have to enrol their racing child into schools that will accommodate and be patient with drivers or in recent times a lot of parents have opted for the home-schooling route.

Education is a personal decision based on your priorities, but as you will have found it is still something that racing can complicate.

Injury

It goes without saying that your child will be exposed to danger whilst racing. We see big accidents in every level of motorsport from karting up, so this is something to take into account and to not ignore.

The majority of drivers make it through their competing years without significant injuries (we are more likely to see people injured in sports like martial arts, horse jumping and motocross) but if it does happen then it can be life-changing and career-ending.

As the parent you should have things in place (like some private medical insurance) because if something does happen then you want the very best chance of recovery and to help your child get back on that 'horse'.

We are in a sport where the highs are seriously high and the lows are seriously low so even though this list of bad things is quite short, they are also quite punchy and hit home just how dedicated you need to be.

The Ugly

Now let's get to the darker side.

Motorsport is a unique sport because most of the relationships within it are temporary.

Take race teams; over the winter period they will look for the drivers they need for the following season only, they are usually thinking short-term and have quite a high turnover of drivers.

As far as drivers are concerned, they too are usually only interested in a certain team for the coming season. Drivers pretty much use teams as a stepping stone for what they want to achieve in their career.

This 'in and out' culture creates an environment where everybody uses one another for short term gain. This is not necessarily a problem, but as a parent you need to understand that things are set up this way. So if you are someone who values long term loyalty, then be prepared to be let down from time to time.

Most people in the paddock have the general outlook of taking what they can today because tomorrow is never guaranteed. Even the mechanics have a saying when it comes to their food each day: "Eat as much as you can now because you never know when your next meal will be."

This is obviously due to how hard they work but still, it's an insight to how motorsport is set up.

People within racing are often in survival mode

Putting things simply: *Teams need cash and results in order to survive, drivers need a good car and a top service in order to thrive. As soon as these ingredients are missing for either, then they look to jump ship where the grass is greener.*

As in many sports we often hear the term: "This is business, it's not personal."

Due to money being the blood that keeps motorsport alive, you have to fully understand this and see things for how they really are.

As far as the ugly side goes, this sets the stage for drivers to feel ripped off at times. So as a parent you really need to be sharp in this area. Teams, managers, coaches and everyone else who is paid to be there all have the potential to mislead you and put their own priorities ahead of yours.

Remember: it's not personal, it is just them playing the game of survival and this can cause people to have the "Screw them before they screw me" mentality.

There are plenty of people in this sport who will genuinely look after you, but for every one of them there are ten people who will serve themselves first.

Again, like the business world, most people are participating selfishly. It doesn't mean they are bad people; it means that they may intentionally or unintentionally hamper your progress as they attempt to meet their own needs.

Either way, as a parent, this is yet another truth that you should remind yourself of.

Bad luck

Another ugly aspect of the sport is down to Lady Luck.

You can do all things right on and off track but due to some unfortunate timing or something out of your control, in the blink of an eye you can be left flat broke and with no future.

To give you examples: due to unforeseeable circumstances your sponsors or race team can suddenly pull the plug on your drive.

Or when a certain person leaves your team or sponsoring partner, you are left with no support and your current opportunity disappears with them.

Or you could sign with the current championship-winning team and have everything in place, only for the team to prioritise your team-mate – so you end up getting the secondary kit and a service that is under par compared to what you expected.

Or a driver can experience a full season of bad luck and mechanical breakdowns, thus tarnishing their reputation and unfairly halting their career.

I'm not even exaggerating here, but I have had drivers in the past who have had seasons where something unfortunate happened at virtually every single race weekend. This then makes them look unfavourable in the industry because nobody believes that one person could have bad luck for so long, but this really does happen from time to time.

Two of the fastest drivers I have ever seen and worked with (who could easily have gone well in F1) had this happen to them and it closed the door to F1 for them. They would have both achieved a lot but instead they had to swallow it and constantly be reminded of what might have been.

That's the ugly side of motorsport, but it is the same for anything we do in life. It's not always the worthy who make it because timing and luck also play a big part in our destiny.

In a nutshell

So that for me is motorsport in a nutshell. It is a tough environment that stresses many areas of your life, whether you are the driver or anyone else who is involved – including you as the parent.

When we step back and take an overview like this we can easily see that your child can take a lot from this experience.

We can also see that it takes a certain mindset and approach in order to succeed in such a sport, so you and your child must understand the level of commitment that this is going to take.

Before we leave this chapter I just want to share a rule that will serve you whether you are just beginning in racing or a seasoned veteran:

There are no guarantees in this sport: you could become world champion or it could all end tomorrow. It will test you every step of the way so fully commit to giving this absolutely everything you have, one day at a time. Also, make sure that you enjoy the ride while it lasts.

CHAPTER 3
THE DIFFERENT PARENTING STYLES

Now we have taken a global look at the industry, it's time for us to continue with a wide-angled lens, but this time I want us to turn our attention to the actual parents in motorsport.

Before we get into this chapter I want to put out a quick disclaimer: *What you are about to read are my observations whilst working in the racing paddocks, I do not intend to mock parents and their parenting styles in any way whatsoever. I have zero judgement when it comes to how people parent their children and will never tell you how to raise yours.*

I wanted to put this disclaimer in because people can misunderstand my intentions here.

My goal here is to simply give you an overview of the different ways in which parents approach things. So let's do just that.

On the sidelines

If you have been to a youth-level football match before, then you will have noticed that the sidelines are littered with parents and they all seem to have their own individual ways of behaving during these matches.

Some parents are shouting instructions to their children, some are praising them, some are quietly watching as they sit back sipping their warm cup of soup, whilst others are hurling abuse at the referee or having punch-ups with other parents.

It's a behavioural expert's dream to people-watch at such events.

I love watching individuals within a group as they provide a variety of reactions to the very same external event. In fact, this is one of my main examples when I am teaching drivers the art of emotional control.

As you will have seen for yourself, this behaviour from Soccer Moms and Dads isn't unique to the world of football; we also get to see this wonderful display of emotions at the race tracks.

Interestingly though, even though we see all these different parenting styles, there doesn't appear to be a right or wrong way of going about things.

We have seen world champions and mentally fulfilled race drivers come from all kinds of different backgrounds and upbringings and raised with every parental style imaginable.

I think it's because it totally depends on the kind of relationship that exists between each parent and child, and how each child responds to their parent's conduct.

Even though we can't say which parenting styles are better, what I can do is share with you the nine common parenting styles that we see in our sport. Here they are:

1. The Stresser Parent
2. The Comforter Parent
3. The Successful Parent
4. The Distant Parent
5. The Overbearing Parent

6. The Bumper Sticker Parent
7. The Opposing Parent
8. The Encouraging Parent
9. The Ex-Racer Parent

The Stresser

This parent is seemingly not happy unless they can find something to stress about; in fact they worry even more if all seems to be going too well. The Stresser will often focus on what is not perfect and the 'worst case scenario'. They could be worrying about things like the team's tyre selection, mistakes their child made on track, the speed trap figures of other drivers or even the weather.

The potential pros of The Stresser parenting style:

- Teams, coaches and managers will make sure they 'tick the boxes' more in order to prevent something going wrong, just to make sure the Stresser's fears do not come to fruition.
- The team may raise their game if they know the parent will be questioning everything and judging their decisions.

The potential cons of The Stresser parenting style:

- It can create a void between the parent and the child because the child needs to remain calm at the track but the parent's mindset disrupts this. You will often see the child getting frustrated with a parent who can't relax at the track. Arguments between them are often started due to this and you will hear the driver say things like "Dad, just chill out, the team have got this" or "Mom, please stop, it will be OK."
- It can also create a tense environment in the race team and put everyone on edge, which then causes people to second-guess their decisions and feel uneasy.

The Comforter

This Comforting Parent will try and keep their child out of harm's way and be a little overprotective. The child only has to cough once and the parent will bring out a bag that could half-stock the local pharmacy. It can easily be argued that parents with this style often do way too much for their children, meaning the children never really need to think for themselves.

The potential pros of The Comforter style:

- Your son or daughter can see how much you love and care for them.
- You will be the person your child comes to when they are upset because they feel comfortable with you.

The potential cons of The Comforter style:

- Not always but often the drivers who have overly comforting parents who do a lot for them, aren't usually thick-skinned enough to take the emotional and physical hits that motorsport dishes out.
- The drivers are not usually self-sufficient because they have been used to their parents doing everything for them. This is not a good trait for a champion to have in sport.

The Successful Parent

Due to this being an expensive sport to compete in, we naturally have a lot of parents who have achieved impressive things in their own right, often in business or other sports. This can obviously be a good thing due to the parent understanding what it takes to succeed. They will have high expectations for what their child can achieve and will put everything in place to help their child progress.

The potential pros of The Successful parenting style:

- The driver will have picked up on some valuable lessons that these parents taught them through their own journey and by the way they act.
- This will understand the lengths that their driver must go through in order to win, so this parent can mentally align with their driver and help if necessary.

The potential cons of The Successful parenting style:

- A Successful Parent can often, like the comforter, do too much for the driver. They may want to save their child from going through the same pain they faced in the early days... but I'm afraid this pain is what makes a champion. If they miss out on the hardship, they often miss the required mindset to succeed in racing.
- The Successful Parent can have unreal expectations and lack of patience for the way the racing world is. We must never ignore that the child might not actually be good enough; you can get quick in a racing car but to be seriously fast and have what it takes to be a champion can often not be taught. Like any other sport, things are not black and white, where you can just throw more money at a challenge to overcome it. Things can take some time.

The Distant Parent

This style of parenting is when we hardly see the parent. They will still be interested in their child's racing but they do not interfere. They will watch from afar and let their kid get on with things. This parent may offer valuable advice but trusts the child to make their own way; what will be will be.

The potential pros of The Distant style:

- The driver has to think for themselves and is often much more self-sufficient, organised and disciplined.

- The driver will tend to make more mistakes, but in doing so they will learn more life skills compared to a driver who has everything done for them.

The potential cons of The Distant style:

- A young driver may miss having that family support and having someone to share the journey with.
- If the driver has no coach with them, they could be taking on too much and their performance may be hampered because of it.

The Overbearing Parent

Opposite to The Distant Parent, this parenting style is when the parent wants to be heavily involved with their child's racing. They may have been hands-on when their child was karting, so they are used to having more influence and control. But as the driver ages and has a race team taking the reins, the parent finds themselves having to take a step back. For various reasons, some parents find this transition difficult.

The potential pros of The Overbearing style:

- This parent can keep the team and others sharper due to their presence at the track.
- Being the parent, nobody else cares as much about your child as you do. Every parent gets this so an Overbearing Parent is at least a person who is genuinely in the driver's corner.

The potential cons of The Overbearing style:

- Your driver can become resentful because their parent/s are too involved and crowding their workplace. The driver may even be embarrassed by the parent being too involved.
- The relationship between the parent and driver is often strained when the parent is on top of them too much.

The Bumper Sticker Parent

These are the parents who use their child's racing as some form of an egotistical trophy. They will be super proud of their children and enjoy saying things like: "My kid is going to be an F1 driver." This is fine and natural by the way, every parent loves to be proud of their children, but the Bumper Sticker Parent will go one step further and wrap up their own sense of self-worth, identity or social status in their child's activities and accomplishments.

Some people explain this as a parent living their own life through their child's racing.

The potential pros of The Bumper Sticker style:

- This parent can actually help get the driver's name out in the paddock more due to how many people they interact with and boast about their child to. They wave the promotional banner for their driver.
- The child may feel more supported by a parent with this style.

The potential cons of The Bumper Sticker style:

- The driver can get embarrassed by the parents when they are constantly bigging them up, and can even start to believe their own hype and become deluded themselves.
- This can cause tension when things are not going to plan and the results are poor. Often Bumper Sticker parents panic and worry about how it makes them look to others.

The Opposing Parent

Opposing Parents would prefer their child not to race. They are against it and would prefer their child to 'get a real job' or focus on education. They may or may not go to the races but are just hoping that racing is just a phase. This often means the driver must make their own way with very little assistance from the parents.

The potential pros of The Opposer style:

- The driver can take the lack of self-belief his or her parents have, and use that to feed their hunger to prove people wrong. When people do not believe in you or your path, that can wake up something inside.
- If the parent/s are opposed to their child racing, yet the driver still goes for it, this is a good sign that they are serious about the sport and that they are at least creating a life they are genuinely passionate about.

The potential cons of The Opposer style:

- The child can feel alone and may turn to the wrong people for advice.
- Later in life the parent may regret being this way and for not supporting their child with their dream.

The Encouraging Parent

The Encouraging Parent is the parent who feeds their child with confidence. They may or may not be present at the tracks much, but they are super-supportive and help their young one believe in themselves. They will say things like "You can achieve anything you want" and "Dream big".

The potential pros of The Encourager style:

- It can feed the confidence of the young driver.
- It helps your driver think bigger and take more chances for their career. Many good things can happen when a child believes in possibility.

The potential cons of The Encourager style:

- The outlook of the driver can cross the line from self-belief into self-delusion. They can ignore their shortcomings when it comes to their skill level and think that just believing in something is enough.

- The child may rely on their parent's encouragement too much – so when motorsport gods decide to dish out some adversity, and they are alone, they could mentally crumble.

The Ex-Racer Parent

This is the parent who has had a racing career of their own before introducing their child to the sport.

The potential pros of The Ex-Racer parent:

- The child won't have to keep translating everything into layman's terms for the parent to understand what is going on. The parent gets exactly what the driver is going through.
- The Ex-Racer Parent often knows what to look for in teams or within their driver's driving – and the pitfalls to avoid.

The potential cons of The Ex-Racer parent:

- If the parent was successful in racing the driver can struggle with creating their own brand or identity in the industry. They may be under the shadow cast by their parent – and this can have many ramifications.
- The Ex-racer Parent could sometimes get carried away with the emotions racing provides, and forget that it is now their child's turn to race and make their own mistakes.

This list

As you can see by this generalised list we have quite a few approaches from parents and I am pretty certain that you could name even more styles.

You may look at this list and guess which style you fall into, but in all honesty, I think most people actually fall into more than just one.

You may lean partially towards 'The Successful' parent and also be part 'The Involver', or you could be an interesting mix between 'The Ex-Racer' and 'The Opposer'. This pairing certain makes for interesting discussions with your driver over dinner... I think I may have just described myself there!

The point I am making here is that there are many different characters within our racing paddocks. Some are more helpful than others when it comes to aiding their child's racing, but each type of parent has something in common: they all want the best for their child/children.

It's just the way each parent goes about it that differentiates them.

World champions of the past

Like I said earlier, there are no right or wrong ways to parent a race driver because there are too many variables involved. World champions of the past have collectively had parents who adopt all of these parenting styles.

For example, we all know the parenting style that Jos Verstappen had with Max. I worked in the same team as Max when he was competing in Formula 3 so I saw it all first-hand. And even though some say that Jos was way too aggressive, from what I have seen so far, his style helped carve Max into one of the quickest and well-rounded drivers we have ever seen.

Time will obviously tell if Max is fulfilled as an individual and happy in his own skin, but for now things look like things are working out for him.

I'm not saying it was the best way to parent a child, but certain elements of how Jos approached things certainly helped Max become the driver he is now.

I fully respect the dedication and commitment Jos had for his son and how they both rewrote the rule book for how to get to F1. Jos was very involved and obviously an ex-racer himself so he fully understood what it took to succeed in this sport.

Jos was skilled mechanically too; he used to build Max's kart engines himself and he definitely knew how to build a fast race car. Couple this with Max's driving skills and you have a formidable team.

Milton da Silva, however, took a different approach when it came to parenting his son, Ayrton Senna. Milton adopted more of the 'Distant' style. When I say Distant I don't mean he didn't care; in fact he was a super supporter of his son. But he wasn't present much at the track due to him having to run the family business in Brazil, so he let Ayrton run his own show over in Europe.

Milton originally wanted Ayrton to run the family business (so he was probably an Opposer in the early days) but when he saw Ayrton's passion for the sport and the results Ayrton was achieving, he couldn't stop his son from pursuing his dream. So he went on to support him as much as he could.

Talking of family businesses, Niki Lauda's parents took the parenting styles of 'The Successful' and 'The Opposers'.

Due to their business background (and with the family living under the shadow of Niki's successful grandfather Hans Lauda, who served as the president for the Federation of Austrian Industries) Niki's parents disapproved of his decision to become a race driver instead of working within the business world.

This for me is what made Niki Lauda so impressive; because if his family had supported him then due to their connections and financial wealth, he could have had quite a straightforward route to F1, but instead he had to turn his back on his family and go it alone. Niki had to hustle like crazy in order to create a career, and that he did.

So here we have three very different parenting styles, yet the talent of each driver shone through and they all achieved great things in our sport.

It just goes to show that no matter what parenting style you find yourself using, it isn't always the determining factor for whether a driver will make it or not, or for how they will turn out in life. Their own character, goals, perspective and mental model of the world will often shine through no matter how you parent them. As a parent you can influence the way they are and the way they act in public, but they get the final say on things.

What I am trying to say here is that it isn't clear-cut for how best to raise your child.

Any parent who has raised multiple kids will tell you that. You can bring all of your kids up the exact same way with the same rules – yet due to their personalities and nature, they can have completely different characters and natural abilities.

My parents

For me I would say my father was The Opposer and my mother was the Encourager. This made for an interesting balance, especially when they got divorced.

On the one hand my father said things like "Racing is not for people like us, it is for the wealthy!" or "What happens if you don't make it and you have missed out on getting a good education?"

Which by the way, used to make me even more determined to go for it and prove him wrong. I have always got a kick out of living a life that isn't 'normal' so I had no fear of my racing not working out. That's because I wanted to chase something that I was passionate about and do something that made me feel alive.

As soon as I fell in love with racing, I fell out of love with school and I wasn't interested in anything that wasn't helping me towards becoming a race driver.

My mother on the other hand would say things like "Go for it" and "Chase that dream darling". I think she was probably the one who convinced my father to help pay for my race licence course when I was 17 years old. I'll tell you this story later in the book...

In some ways I can say that racing helped change my life and I feel so lucky that my parents helped me on the way to this.

So I was driven to succeed by my father's initial pessimism and spurred on by my mother's encouragement. For me this created a great balance that would give me drive and fuel my mindset. I was already motivated to go racing, but this was the icing on the cake.

The funny thing is, due to racing I stumbled upon my true passion of performance psychology. Since the late Nineties I have been obsessed with this field – and if it wasn't for my time in motorsport, I may have never realised this.

While I was competing I always searched for ways in which to improve my personal performance so it wasn't long before I became fascinated with the self-help industry. I ended up absorbing as much information as I could in relation to self-development.

From there I became a qualified Life Coach and began coaching people inside and outside of motorsport. I soon realised that coaching was giving me more fulfilment and purpose than racing did so it wasn't long before I hung up my helmet and pursued my career as a performance coach.

This is another good thing about motorsport and chasing your dreams in general: you end up finding your way.

Thanks to my parents I found mine, and thanks to you, your child will find theirs.

CHAPTER 4
THE TOP CHALLENGES THAT PARENTS FACE

We have already touched upon the arduous job that you and other racing parents have, but now I want to move away from being empathetic to your situation and kick things up a gear so we can begin to tackle the challenges that you face.

We will do this by first becoming clear on what I see as the common challenges that you will either currently have – or will have in the future – as you navigate your way through this sport.

To make things simple I will split the challenges into two sections to help you compartmentalise things and again lay things out as if this was a troubleshooting guide.

First we will look at the challenges that I see parents having with their boy and girl racers in terms of their personal performance, and the second part of this book will be dedicated to the career related challenges that parents often face.

Here we go...

Driver performance challenges

In this first part we will cover the personal performance issues that arise when your driver is not meeting expectations or not achieving the results that they could be (not reaching their potential).

Whilst talking about this topic we must remember that age plays quite a big factor when it comes to their development. Even though it can be super-frustrating to watch them underachieve compared to their potential, we need to remind ourselves that they may not be seeing things from our perspective yet.

We would love them to have the correct mindset and the required professional approach but in reality it is often not the case. So we need to help them and coach them into becoming the person they need to become in order to succeed.

Before we get into that, let's look at the most common things that I hear parents say when describing the challenge that they are facing:

- "He has no work ethic or discipline"
- "She is taking too long to improve"
- "He can't control his emotions on track"
- "She can test well but when it comes to qualifying, she hardly ever delivers"
- "He needs more confidence as a person"
- "He gets too moody and drops his head after a bad result"
- "He is more interested in his girlfriend and mates than his racing"

I'm sure that you have said more than one of these in the past.

Well, welcome to the club. Many other parents, team managers and coaches have also muttered the same words so you are far from being alone here.

We will address all these areas in the first part of the book.

Career challenges

In Part 2 we will turn our attention to the kind of challenges parents experience when it comes to their child's career or racing in general. These are the kinds of statements and questions that we hear parents say in this area:

- "I don't know what career path to choose and don't want to make the wrong choice"
- "How do I know which team is the best fit for us?"
- "Do we need a manager?"
- "We are running out of money, what can we do?"
- "The race team are simply not performing well enough"
- "How do I know if my kid has what it takes?"
- "Why is my son not getting the breaks he deserves?"

These concerns – which are often voiced – cover most of the main things that must be dealt with if your driver is to progress in the sport.

Going forward

I have dedicated a chapter to each of these challenges. So from this point forward feel free to skip to the most relevant chapters for you and your driver.

For the rest of this book I will mainly refer to your child as 'your driver' and give you the most up-to-date advice that I can offer.

Having said that, if you are going to skip chapters, I recommend that you first read the next chapter because I will give you the blueprint of what I see as the most important attributes that your driver should work on if they want to become a champion in this sport.

PART 2:

MENTAL PERFORMANCE TRAINING

CHAPTER 5
THE 5 TRAITS OF A CHAMPION

To kick off the driver performance section of this book I want to outline what it takes for a driver to be a champion in motorsport. The traits I will highlight here are the kind of traits that all top drivers share, so if you want to help your driver perform better it's fairly important for me to explain what an elite level driver looks like.

I am not telling you this so we can sit back and marvel at other drivers. Instead I want you to know all the key traits that really separate drivers who are destined to achieve great things in our sport compared to those who will forever struggle.

Put simply; we can improve our own game by learning from those who have successfully walked the path before us.

It's a mental war

Winning in sport is a lot like winning on the battlefield, hence why I wrote the book *The Warrior's Mind.*

For me the most important skill a driver can possess is their ability to use their mind effectively and train it with skills that are specific for their racing. Pretty much all of my coaching is based on helping drivers create the Racing Brain so they are internally coded in a way that helps them get the most from themselves.

It's my aim to help drivers design their mental programming so it fits the task in hand and gives them that competitive advantage. They need to arm themselves with the knowledge and skills required to perform on demand – all while dealing with the constant barrage of hurdles they face both on and off the track.

If they can go some way to mastering their inner world, then things in their external world will often fall into place.

Due to my viewpoint on this, you will notice that most of the qualities that I cover in this chapter refer to a race driver's mental abilities, as well as their outlook on life. That's because time and time again I see this area as being the biggest differentiator.

Top drivers are not necessarily the quickest drivers all the time but they operate in a way that helps them consistently deliver. They have a mental model (a Matrix) that gives them the traits that I will now talk about.

Here is the shortlist of what I consider the most important traits – beyond their actual driving skills – that true champions in our sport tend to possess.

No.1 - They are willing to risk it all

To put it bluntly, top performing drivers seem to have very little thought for the consequences that their actions may create. They hardly ever hesitate when in the heat of a battle, they allow their natural instinct and subconscious mind to react for them. By operating in this way they often make decisions that serve them and they are able to mentally flow.

Drivers who are able to perform in this way don't usually take the time to ask the "What if...?" questions that most other drivers do.

So when they are turning into a blind corner in the wet at 120 mph (193 km/h) they won't be thinking of the concrete wall that is dangerously close to the exit; instead they will only be thinking about driving that corner as fast as they can.

As they try to overtake someone, they will instinctively go for the gap on the outside that is barely wide enough for their car to fit. Sometimes it works and sometimes it doesn't – but they won't take the time to consciously weigh the risks up. Instead they spot a possible move and act immediately.

In their eyes these risky situations are not risky at all; they see these moments as opportunities to be the fastest or to take the win. They will happily go toe-to-toe with danger because for them it's completely normal when you are searching for the limits or in a fight.

To achieve this perspective the driver must have the sort of mental coding that allows them to view things in this way, then they will be able to perform with less friction.

No.2 - They have high standards

When I say this I mean that they have high standards for what they expect from themselves, from their team, from their car and from anyone or anything that can influence the outcome in some way.

They don't take shortcuts and they are very proactive. No stone is left unturned when they are competing and they expect everyone around them to approach things in the same way.

This can lead to heated discussions with their team members, but the driver is usually excused because everyone understands the level at which they work, and what is expected if you are to work with them.

Even as a coach, if I am working with someone who has an impressive work ethic and high standards then I automatically raise mine. Their work ethic and desire to succeed is infectious, plus you don't want to let them down by being the weaker link.

By the way, this also works the other way. If I have a lazy driver who won't do anything for himself or herself, then I also can't help but give less myself.

When you work with a driver who has these high standards it is often like trying to tame a beast, but once the dust settles you soon realise the amount of fulfilment that you got by being a part of it all. They drain you of everything you have, but the memories and shared moments are worth it.

When Gordon Ramsay first hit our TV screens back in the Nineties with his fly-on-the-wall programmes, you would see him shouting at everyone and demanding a lot from his staff. It was the epitome of the saying: "If you can't stand the heat, get out of the kitchen."

Ramsay reminds me of what it's like to work with a true champion. They are one of the best at what they do, so you'd better keep up and match them otherwise you will slow the whole machine down.

I'm pointing all of this out because not only does this approach to having a high standard help the driver improve their skills, it also helps everyone else apply themselves and ensures that you have the right people working with you.

No.3 - Their hunger to win drives them to study their craft

When a racing vehicle (no matter what it is) is being driven on a knife-edge and completely on the limit, you can describe it as being partially out of control.

One gust of wind, one slightly large piece of gravel laying on the surface or one small mistake from the driver can result in that vehicle leaving the track and rolling itself into a ball on top of a barrier.

The thing with race drivers is that they are often control freaks. They like to take something that is seemingly out of control and tame it to do what they want.

When you have a sport that has as many variables as motorsport and you put control freaks in it, you will find them becoming fascinated in all the aspects that could possibly help them control the outcome more.

This means that a top driver often finds themselves going deeper into their craft compared to most other drivers. They take the time to study the onboard videos, the data, the engineering aspects and anything else that they can use to help them understand things more.

Of course they are also feeding their hunger for doing whatever it takes to win, but essentially they don't like it when they feel they don't have much of a say in the result. They want to study as much as they can to influence the outcome.

Put simply, they care more than the average driver. It means more to them and this is their way of doing everything in their power to be at their best.

To use two very typical examples, Ayrton Senna and Michael Schumacher both showed the lengths that they would go to in order to get the best out of themselves, their car and their teams. They went the extra mile and wanted to understand it all.

Again, from my own experience, if I am sharing a room or a car journey with a driver with the traits and makings of a true champion, I will know it. I will hear the constant noise of an engine revving as they watch different onboard videos and we will stay up late into the night talking about racing.

When I hear a driver doing this, it makes me smile inside because I know they are dedicated and into studying their craft. An essential ingredient for a champion.

No.4 - They learn and apply things fast

This one impresses the hell out of me and it's a trait that is plain for everyone to see: it's a driver's ability to learn quickly and get on the pace immediately.

I don't mean on a normal test day when they are driving a car they are already familiar with. I mean when a driver is testing a car that is new to them, yet within the first ten minutes on track they are already posting competitive lap times.

There are only a handful of times that I have witnessed this, but when a driver outperforms their expectations I like to call this a Stopwatch Moment. This happens when you are timing a driver with a stopwatch and as that driver passes you, you hit the lap button on the stopwatch, you look down at the time and you are completely stunned.

When this happens I usually doubt myself and think I must have pressed the button too early or something. So when they next drive by I make sure I get the timing spot on, only to see that the time I originally got was in fact correct, and they pump out yet another outrageous time. That's me having my Stopwatch Moment.

It feels like the script of a movie when this happens.

Top drivers can do this because they have such a great sense for what a car feels like when it is on the limit and they take the car there. They figure out what driving style works for that particular car before anyone needs to tell them. Obviously they still improve their driving over time but instead of coming into the pits and being taught how to brake correctly, they are immediately working on the minor details of the driving.

The most recent time I experienced this was with a driver competing in FIA F3 at Spa. Even though he was over halfway through the championship (so he knew his car well), he was turning up to the Spa F1 race event having never been there before. He hadn't even been to Spa as a spectator.

He obviously knew the circuit layout from driving it on the simulator but even so, it was a big ask for him to be competitive in the early stages of the weekend. That especially applies when you are competing in a championship where you only get about eight push laps in free practice, before going straight into qualifying.

However, he gave me my Stopwatch Moment. On the very first push lap he was P1. Then on the second push lap he again went P1.

This wasn't competing against a grid of drivers who had never been there either; most of them had raced and tested at that track many times before. It was impressive.

I stood at Pouhon (a challenging high speed corner) because I thought this would be the toughest corner for him to get right, yet on lap one he was visibly quicker than every single one of the other 29 drivers on that grid.

I had to shake my head and tip my hat to him because that's what it takes if you want to become a top level driver.

When you step up into F1 for the free practice role as a rookie driver they don't care whether it is your first time in an F1 car and they don't care that it is your big moment. They simply expect you to drive the car as well as their regular drivers, immediately. There is no real 'getting used to it' period.

So for me this is a big quality that a driver needs if they want to make it big in this sport.

If your child is struggling here, please spend time training them in this area. Make it a priority because not only is it essential to have this ability but if done correctly then it will speed up their overall learning process.

After all, being fast is the name of the game.

No.5 - They are very coachable

Due to the technology we have now, a driver is constantly shown where and how they can improve their driving, so knowing what to improve is hardly ever the problem.

The problems come when drivers:

1. Have an outlook that causes them not to want to listen to advice
2. Find it hard to apply the changes that have been suggested

Whether it is an ego-related reason or they lack the ability to apply the required changes on the go, they hit a 'performance ceiling' where we see their progress plateau.

When a driver is coachable they listen intently and immediately try what the engineer or driver coach has advised them to do. A coachable driver is always open to changing things and wants to understand how they can extract more from themselves or the car. They do not take critical feedback personally; they just want to improve.

To give you another real world example of this, I once went to a big kart race at the PFI circuit in the UK to meet the Verstappens. That's because I was working for the Lotus F1 Junior Program and quite simply we were trying to sign Max up to our programme.

Max was competing so I watched him on track. After one of his sessions I went into his pit garage to show him what some of the other front-runners were doing on a particular corner compared to him. I cannot even remember what I was showing him but what I do remember was how intently he was listening. He looked me straight in the eyes with interest because he was eager to learn something new. He then went out in the next session and gave it a go.

This stuck with me because he didn't really know me at that point – all he knew was that I was from a junior academy and I wanted to meet him – but still his interest in possibly finding something out was good to see.

You could see he was used to taking on information and he had no problem applying new things. Now that's what I call being coachable.

It's not all sunshine and rainbows

I'm sure you have seen many more traits that top drivers have but these are my main ones. Having said all this, we can easily get carried away as we big-up these drivers so it's only right to stress that things are not all sunshine and rainbows when it comes to top level drivers.

Quite apart from how difficult these drivers can be to work with, we must also understand that just because a driver is considered a great, it doesn't mean they are great at everything.

Sometimes the genius of any sport or other disciplines can be driven by their insecurities and fears which leads them to a life of unfulfillment. We often see the greats letting their emotions get the best of them, or times when they struggle to deal with everyday life.

Top race drivers may be able to perform on demand at a circuit, driving in a way that leaves us all gobsmacked. But let's not forget that there are other factors that contribute towards the whole picture and very rarely do we see a driver who has everything in place.

That's because they are human, and as with all humans they have their weaknesses.

Use this information

The real reason I am telling you all this is because I want to bring to your attention the blueprint for what makes a top driver so you can start to benchmark your driver and help them create their own self-development plan.

Self-awareness and discovering the truth about a driver's current level is a critical starting point when helping them to improve their results.

To start this process off, let me ask you something. If you take the five attributes I've mentioned, and you were to subjectively score your driver from 1 - 10 in each area, how would they score?

To give you a reminder of the areas, they were:

No.1 - They are willing to risk it all

No.2 - They have high standards

No.3 - Their hunger to win drives them to study their craft

No.4 - They learn and apply things fast

No.5 - They are very coachable

If you do the math and add up the individual scores for each area, how do they fair against the top score of 50?

This is a very simplified version of what I actually do with drivers when coaching them. I like to know what strengths and skills are required to be in place if they are to reach their chosen goal, then I assess where they score in the relevant areas.

Once you have a rough idea of where your driver is at, then you can start to build a training plan that helps them raise their scores.

I'll explain this more later in the book, but for now this can act as a good starting point for you to seek out the truth and understand what needs to be done.

A big part of this book is making you fully aware of what it takes for a driver to succeed. By sharing these traits you can start to benchmark your driver and monitor their progress going forward.

CHAPTER 6
MY KID WON'T LISTEN TO ME

Whether in racing or not, when your child gets to a certain age, communication between you and your child can become a challenge. They no longer open up to you and they can be difficult to get through to.

I am sure that you have either been a part of or witnessed a very similar conversation to this in the car during the school run:

Parent: Hello Johnny.

Child: Hi.

Parent: How was school today?

Child: Fine.

Parent: So what did you get up to, did anything interesting happen?

Child: No, normal stuff.

Parent: Ah OK... well what do you want for dinner tonight?

Then the child proceeds to put in their earbuds and you lose them to their phone.

What, really?

It has been some time since I was at school but from what I remember there was actually quite a lot that can happen on any given day, especially at an age where being popular is the number one currency and you are sensitive to the way others behave.

If a child actually told the truth and filled you in with what they went through at school, you would hear things like:

> *"I forgot my shorts so I had to do gym class using someone else's smelly shorts that I picked out from the Lost & Found box. The other kids teased me and I cried."*
>
> *"Natasha in my maths class passed me a note today, I think she likes me."*
>
> *"Ollie dropped the test tube in science and made the whole room smell like a fart."*
>
> *"Simon Drake purposely knocked my pencil case off my desk so my stationary went everywhere, people started to kick them around the room and I ended up getting told off for it by the teacher."*
>
> *"I got a B for my metal workshop project."*
>
> *"James Potter stole Bobby's lunch today so I shared my lunch with him."*

When you have a building full of hundreds of kids in various age groups, stuff is always going down. There is always some gossip.

What makes it even funnier is when they (especially as they get older) sum up a whole seven-hour day of school with the single word: "Fine".

This isn't a case of schools getting boring now, instead it's a case of the communication breakdown that happens between most children and their parents. You know for sure that if their friend was to ask them the same question about their day (instead of the parent) that same child would give a blow-by-blow account and there would be plenty of stories to tell.

I am sure that at some point, you remember doing the same thing to your parents. You just couldn't be bothered to explain things to them because they would either not get it or they would offer their judgement/advice about things, which you just don't want to hear because they don't understand.

Well I'm afraid it is now your turn to be that parent who gets this kind of treatment. This is just how children see things.

When this is happening, please remember this is not personal and they still love you. It's just the kid growing up and having their own mind. It is just another phase they go through.

You should consider yourself lucky if you do not have this communication challenge. Be grateful that you have a child who opens up and shares things with you – because from what I have seen, most parents do not have this luxury.

This is not easy

Being a parent in this situation can be difficult to digest because when your child was born and during their formative years, you were their entire world. They depended on you for everything, they demanded your attention and you were essential for their survival.

However, as they grow (especially when they are in their teenage years) they behave in a way that makes you feel less significant in some ways.

As human beings one of our most desired needs is 'significance'. Whether this is in our relationships, within our social circles or at work, we crave the need to be liked, loved or significant in some way. Even the angry boss in the workplace or the thug on the street who seem to thrive off being feared by others, are actually ticking their Significance Box.

Something interesting happens, though. As children develop they start to look for other ways to gain significance. So instead of just crying to be fed and loved, they start to demonstrate that they are all grown up and they no longer need to be guided by their parents.

So when a parent expresses their opinions on something they are doing, they view that as their parent knocking their significance in some way.

All of this makes for interesting times – and depending on how your child handles this phase, they will either talk to you more to prove their worth or they will shut you out to show they can do this on their own.

They have the same goal (to earn your love and respect) but each child goes about this in their own way.

As you can imagine I find this fascinating to watch and play out. Human behaviour is my passion, so seeing all this unfold with my clients is something I like to help with in some way.

You see this breakdown in communication between parents and their children at circuits because the drivers are normally at an age when they really want to be their own person and they detest it when their parents tell them what to do.

Their newly-formed ego kicks in at the track and they seem to listen to everyone else in the paddock apart from their own parents. It sounds rude and obnoxious of them to do this, but it is just a sign of them growing up and figuring things out.

I hear your pain here because it's not nice when your relationship changes with your children. But instead of letting this worry you, let's come up with a plan for handling this and for getting through to your child.

Same thing, different person

Every driver coach will tell you there are often times when they are giving their driver the exact piece of advice or feedback the driver's parents did previously, but due to the advice coming from the coach, the child happily receives it.

Yet when their mother or father previously gave them that very same piece of advice, the child seemingly rejected it.

I see this a lot. I am often echoing what the driver's parents are saying but because it's coming from me, they take it.

Engineers, team bosses and personal trainers will share the same observation. It is common to hear a frustrated parent say something like: "Hey coach, will you tell him because he'll listen to you?"

When you hear a parent say this, you just know that they are experiencing the usual communication challenge.

So first off I want you to be aware that this is completely normal and all part of the game. You are not alone.

They want to impress you

The important thing to remember is not to take this personally – and to think back to when you were their age and how you might have done the same to your parents at some point.

One of the main reasons children do this is because you are actually the one person who they want to impress the most in this world.

If you ask people who they want to make proud, more often than not they will point to their parents – or at least one of them.

Due to you being the one person they want to prove something to, you will often be the last person they want to take advice from. That's because they want to do it themselves and make you proud.

This behaviour and goal of theirs started way back in their early lives as babies, when they would scream to get your full attention. Then as they grew up you can see their tactics changed. In first school they wouldn't scream and cry any more, instead they would paint you a picture in class. As they painted that picture, all they would be thinking about is your reaction as they revealed it to you, it motivated them.

When you pick them up from school that day they tell you they painted it all by themselves and they would be hoping you receive it with a huge "Wooow... that is amazing, thank you sweetheart, you are so good at painting." Then you would stick it to the fridge or up on the wall.

Since these early days they understood they can cause that kind of reaction from you and get your love and attention.

They carry that through to their career and their relationships and they think of you each time they make a decision in life. In some way, this behaviour usually carries on into their adult life.

So I want you to always remember this...

If you are too involved and help them too much, then in their eyes, they may see that as you taking the credit away from them.

It's a super-twisted situation because you love your child/children with your whole heart so you want to help and share the journey with them. Yet because they love you and care about what you think of them, they push you away.

This is the parent/child tug of war that is fascinating to watch from my perspective – because all I see is just how much you both love each other. Yet somehow both parties don't quite know how to communicate that.

It's not easy when two minds want the same thing, even if their way of going about it differs. But that's life: it's just your child figuring things out so they won't necessarily go about things as you want them to. Their young mind doesn't see things like yours does and your viewpoint will most likely differ from theirs at this time.

If your parents are still alive then I bet from time to time you still do this now. They will offer their advice on something in your working or personal life and you will either fight it or think: "Argh, you don't understand!"

That might still be you thinking that you want to handle things alone and prove to them that you've got this. Some things never change, right?

How to tackle this

We could write a whole new book on this topic alone, and I'm sure there are plenty out there. But for now I want to give you some tips on what I have seen work with this challenge.

First, we must spell out the actual problem...

The problem: We have a child who is pursuing something that's important to them. As their parent you can see things they are getting wrong or things they could do better, so you want to help them improve. After all, that's part of a parent's job.

However, the child wants to be their own person and stand on their own two feet. They want to impress you more than anyone else on this planet – but when you offer your advice they see it as nagging, encroaching or they think you don't understand.

An answer: First of all I suggest you align with and understand their viewpoint, then from there you can communicate accordingly.

If you hear two kids who are friends chatting, they are hardly ever telling each other to tidy up their room, clean up after themselves or get their homework done before going on the PlayStation.

I'm not saying you are incorrect for saying these things to your children, because you need to teach them how to be organised and instil discipline. But due to this (in your child's eyes) you are more of a disciplinarian rather than a mate. So when you say something to your child about their driving or offer them some gentle advice, they will put you in a frame similar to that of a teacher at school, and receive your comments that way.

By the way, this is all on top of what I previously said about you being the one person they want to prove something to.

That's why when some advice is offered by a coach or an engineer, the child takes it in because they see that particular person as their experienced member of staff who is there to help them improve. So the child receives their words in that frame.

By contrast, you have told your child/children what to do for most of their lives. So when they start to become their own person you can understand why (like we did when we were growing up) they don't want to receive that advice from you. If anything, they fight it.

It is a slight attitude problem that children often have but it's just the way things are. So we need to understand that and (unless they are being downright rude to you) let it go. Then we can focus on how to communicate better with them.

Give them the reins

Even though it isn't pleasant when your beloved child constantly fights against what you tell them, instead of letting this situation frustrate you, how about we change the way things are set up?

For example, if you feel they are doing this because they have reached a certain age when they want to be their own person and take the reins... then let them.

Make it clear to them that they are now the ones who are in control – and trust them to make their own way, whatever that will be. This doesn't mean that you cut them off and never help them, it just means that you will be less on their back about the minor things and see how things go.

There comes a time when less assistance from the parents actually speeds progress up and you get to find out if they will actually sink or swim.

You will always be there to prevent them from sinking at the last moment. But giving them more space to lead things and take on more responsibility can either help them grow up quicker, or they will come crawling back to you for advice and assistance.

If they do come crawling back, then at least they will do it on their terms and they will be more open to your contribution.

This can be with the small things first, like not reminding them they need to eat or drink halfway through the test day, folding their clothes up in the truck or telling them to smile.

By the way, as I coach I also have to stop myself from doing some of the small things for drivers. As soon as I notice I am starting to nag about the small things, I focus on the bigger. more important aspects – because we only have so much time and focus. So you are not alone here.

If you don't do this, you will be the person who is constantly nagging the driver. This is the last thing they need during a race weekend when they are already going through a lot mentally as they worry about their actual performance.

Once again, I am all for discipline and the 'make your bed in the morning' approach. Yet while it is one thing – and normal – to nag your child at home, to keep this same dynamic going at the track is never a good thing.

The biggest thing to remember is that when your child is at home, it's your child within your domain. But when a child is at the track, they are a racing driver within their domain.

It is their workplace.

Your relationship with your child has to change and become more professional when you are at the track. A driver at a track is equivalent to you being at work. They have to become someone different from who they are when at home.

They are on show when they're at the track. They are on their stage so if they still have their parents criticising them in their arena it doesn't help anything. The dynamic of the parent/child relationship style has to change when it's game time.

So taking a step back and letting them run with their flaws – maybe one day forgetting their gloves because they were the ones who packed their kit bag for once – is often the best way for them to advance and become responsible.

Usually the drivers with the most helpers or outside assistance are the ones who take the longest to grow up, and in many cases they lack the personal skills required for them to become the champion.

Work ethic is a topic for the next chapter, but it is also related to what we are talking about here. By letting the driver be the one who runs things, and ensuring that we (as parents or coaches) do not major on the minor things, it helps everyone set their own boundaries. As a result, communication improves.

Enter their inner world

To improve any relationship, we have to see things through the eyes of the other person. We need to understand how they are translating things in their mind and how they will process our words.

Once we do this, we can adjust our communication to suit and not talk to them just using our own model of the world.

This is as relevant between parent and child as it is between husband and wife.

How to kick things off

It may be difficult to make a sudden change to this way of interacting with your son or daughter. So what I have found works best when needing to adjust things in the communication department is to have a heart-to-heart Sit Down.

In the next chapter I will mention this again... but if you can get your child alone, in a relaxed environment where you can both be uninterrupted and focus on the conversation, then you can start to address things in the best way.

This doesn't mean in the car when you are more focused on the road and they are busy scrolling through social media. This is a time when you are away from all technology and distractions and have each other's full attention.

It may be a good idea to set the mood also, to make sure their mind is aligned with what you want to talk about.

Depending on what you do as pastimes, this can be during a hike, on a boat fishing or in a restaurant after watching an inspirational movie at the cinema. You want to speak to them when their guard is down and they are in a calm mood.

Then you use this time to align with them mentally, to explain how proud you are of them for what they have achieved up to now and that you can see they have all it takes to achieve whatever they want in this life.

What you say next is completely individual to your situation... but on a global scale all you need to get across to them is that they are the person who is to make things happen.

You will always be there for them but the only person who can really achieve what they want, is themselves.

If you feel that you, as a parent, have been too overbearing and controlling over them, explain how you will take a step back now and be less intrusive. You don't want them to think that you are being moody and abandoning them, instead you want them to realise that you are backing them all the way but trusting them to take the reins.

If you feel you haven't helped them enough, ask them if there is anything they need to improve themselves and anything they need from you.

If you have noticed that they don't respect you and they are harsh in their words when talking to you, use this moment to kindly find out why. Doing this correctly by aligning yourself with them can be a complete game-changer in the relationship.

All you want to do is help your child. But it just needs to be communicated in a way that allows them to see that. Even if this one initial talk doesn't work and it turns into an argument, at least you have started the ball rolling. It will only be a matter of time before they 'get it'.

If you can achieve all this while explaining that you will always be there for them but it's time for them to step up, they will eventually start to show appreciation and be more receptive to when you do offer your advice.

You must follow through

Once you have done the 'Sit Down' – and hopefully it was received well – the hard part starts. You have to maintain this approach.

This means that when you're back at the race circuit, you fight the urge to fall back into old ways and overreact when they slip up.

Obviously they will need a verbal clip round the ear from time to time, that's normal, but when it comes to their racing it's important to let them lead things.

As you can imagine, there is a balance here and each driver is different. But if you strike the correct balance of how involved you are with what they actually require, then you and your child can create a formidable partnership.

The best parent/child relationships I have seen are the ones where the parent is super-supportive but doesn't take over and steal the thunder from the driver.

In my opinion the ideal relationship is when the parent has high expectations for what their child can achieve, but still lets the child know that whether they win or lose, they love them no matter what.

As Kobe Bryant said: ***"My father just gave me a hug and said 'Listen, whether you score 0 or you score 60, I'm gonna love you no matter what.'"***

Kobe said this gave him the confidence to be himself and give it everything – because he no longer feared failure. He realised that the love from his father was not conditional and it didn't depend on the results he achieved.

That's big for a child.

This gives your child the permission to work hard and give it their all with no pressure of not being enough. If a person with skill has this outlook, then you just watch them fly.

The balance of helping them see this is the big challenge – but that is the overriding goal and role of a parent. The parent needs to energise their child and motivate them while helping them learn the life skills that are required.

Getting the right people in place

If after all this you decide to take more of a back seat to allow your child to shine, as a quick word of advice please make sure you have the right people around your driver.

This could be in the form of a good race team – where the team boss actually respects and looks after your child – or a good coach or trainer to be with them.

The driver still needs guidance from their parents but when it comes to their racing, having someone who is specialised (who you both trust) can be the perfect balance and help communication no end.

All in all

To summarise things, when it comes to communicating better with your child, here are the main points to remember:

1. Understand things from their perspective; see it through their eyes
2. Align with them and have the 'Sit Down' to reset the relationship
3. Put them in charge and be prepared to step back
4. Be there for them and let them know that you love them no matter what
5. If needed, make sure they have a solid personal team or person working with them

You may need to adjust this approach to fit your situation... but hopefully there is at least one sentence within this chapter that has given you some food for thought.

CHAPTER 7
IMPROVE THEIR WORK ETHIC AND DISCIPLINE

This is yet another topic that tops the charts for 'things that parents struggle with'.

It's also the subject that bothers me the most, because there is nothing more frustrating than a driver who cannot be bothered or is not driven enough to put in the necessary work – especially when they have some serious talent.

Our sport is full of drivers who are approaching their sport half-assed. I think this is due to most drivers not being the ones who have to pay for their participation in the sport. Many of them are gifted the chance to race so their need to hustle in order to compete in the first place is not really a thing for them.

Whether they work hard or not, they still get to go racing and be a part of a cool sport which allows them to skip school and play in life.

Yes, these drivers may go down the gym five times per week, but that's not the only kind of work you need to put in if you want to become a professional driver. Fitness is a minor contributing factor towards success in racing.

A certain level of fitness is obviously required in order to drive but there are far more important areas that drivers should be spending their time on.

To give you an example, drivers who are serious about creating or maintaining a career should be spending most of their days doing the following:

- Keeping in regular contact with the race team to ensure progress in all areas and for organisational reasons
- Keeping in regular contact with current sponsors and investors
- Keeping in regular contact with their manager and/or coach
- Taking part in the training sessions or tasks set out by the coach or team
- Proactively preparing as much as they possibly can for each event
- Going over recent tests and races to create their own personal performance system
- Participating in esports events
- Researching and improving their knowledge of race car engineering
- Working on parts of their performance that are below par (mentality, car control, etc)
- Approaching potential sponsors
- Creating or maintaining their brand via social media
- Making relationships with people in the industry or with teams to open up future opportunities
- Maybe working in the industry to earn money and make more contacts
- Learning and using leadership skills so they can drive their team forward
- Keeping up with necessary organisation and paperwork

- Learning useful career-enhancing or personal skills that will help them achieve their racing goals (sales, leadership and entrepreneurial skills)

When a driver is dedicated and motivated to create a career in motorsport, they usually map out what they want to achieve in their racing, then they come up with the plan for how to get there. Next they start to list the things that need to be done so their days are filled with forward-moving tasks like these.

I don't think most drivers realise just how influential their actions are and how their career depends on them. They just think they need to be fast and the rest will sort itself out, but it's not really like that.

There are hundreds of fast drivers out there right now who are more than capable of competing at the top of motorsport, but their work ethic and approach has prevented them from getting there.

If a driver is serious about making it in this sport they literally have to approach their sport as an entrepreneur approaches their career; they have to wear many hats as they battle their way forward and they must steer the ship. It takes daily progress – in all areas – to make a career in motorsport.

With this in mind, a driver should be one of the busiest people in sport due to all the different tasks they have. Yet I think you'll agree this is not how things are in reality.

There's an opportunity here

It's quite rare for drivers (especially younger ones) to put this kind of necessary work in – and that's precisely why we see so many drivers fail to achieve successful careers.

Hindsight is a great thing. But when I talk to drivers who are no longer racing or competing in championships that are beneath their potential, I often quiz them about their approach in the earlier days to see if they would do things differently if they could do it all again.

One hundred percent of the time they are still kicking themselves for how they acted when they were younger, and they regret the lack of application they had back then.

I think we can all say that about some parts of our lives, right?

If we could go back in time too, we would give ourselves a kick up the back side in some areas. However, instead of us living in regret, let's use our own hindsight for educating your driver and helping them apply themselves more.

Two things come to mind as I write this.

First, as the parent, you are in the best position to give your young one the kick up the backside that may be required for them to get their act together, and teach them how to hustle their way forward in the racing world.

Second, due to most drivers having a seriously poor work ethic, you and your driver have an amazing opportunity here. If you are determined to succeed within an industry where most of your competitors are lazy and not learning the necessary skills required for them to succeed, you have the perfect opportunity to clean up and take advantage.

If we can get your son or daughter to fully apply themselves and to give a shit about their racing, they can overtake the other drivers in more ways than one.

Any coach will tell you they would much prefer to work with a driver who may not be the absolute fastest out there but who works their tail off, compared to working with a fast driver who is lazy.

The lazy fast driver simply won't make it to the pinnacle of our sport – or if by some miracle they do, they won't last long there. Yet a driver who may be missing 0.2s per lap compared to the quickest driver on the grid, yet has a strong work ethic, will probably remain valuable to a professional race team. They are likely to have a fruitful career.

I can think of quite a few drivers who did actually spend their days tirelessly working on their racing and all of them (yes, all of them) achieved impressive racing careers. It goes to show that if you approach things in the right way, you massively increase your chances of getting somewhere.

It is so refreshing for a team, manager or coach when they have a driver who is setting the standard due to their impressive work rate; when they are the one banging on doors and pushing themselves on and off track.

People in the sport want to see and work with a driver who has the hunger to make things happen. It inspires us all and we can't help but want to help drivers like this. There are many opportunities that have been given to drivers from professional outfits just because they like the way the driver works, behaves and how they approach their craft.

Never forget that!

So the opportunity here is not just to take advantage of all the other part-time drivers out there, but also to grab the attention of industry leaders by the way your driver applies themselves.

A strong work ethic is visual: people see it, they notice it and it's the kind of reputation your driver needs if they are to peacock themselves in the paddock.

So I really suggest that we make work ethic top priority with your driver – because things just won't happen without it.

If they are not on the pace, they can work hard to make themselves faster.

If they don't have the sponsorship, they can put their business hats on and set things up so they actually can help companies grow through motorsport.

If they are not getting the chances they deserve, they can work on getting in front of those who can offer them opportunities.

It all comes down to this.

Help them see this

We must help your driver see this opportunity and show them how work ethic alone will help them get ahead.

The tricky part for you, as the parent, is that you will need to communicate this without it sounding like you are nagging them.

This is not a case of you constantly being on their back reminding them of all the things they should be doing. Ideally we want your child to be the one who is waking up early to work on their craft or to write a message to someone who can help them.

Instead you need to inspire them to work in the required way and ignite that fire within them. It's easier said than done but you know them better than anyone else on this planet so I am sure you can brainstorm and experiment with ways for doing this.

Every decent parent wants to help their child become self-sufficient and teach them how to look after themselves when it's their turn to carry the torch. A parent is obviously not going to be around forever so we need to ensure that our children are able to lead their own lives and create the future they want.

It's a parent's responsibility to create the foundations that help their children do this. The quicker we help them do that, the better.

This obviously goes beyond racing alone; it's essentially their path to success no matter what they turn their hand to. They need to fully apply themselves to everything that is important to them, even their relationships.

The process for creating work ethic

Drivers are never too young (or too old) to improve their work ethic, but if they are lacking in this area then we obviously need to help them.

Work ethic is a topic that has as many variables as motor racing itself, and the effectiveness of what I will advise in this chapter can be further influenced by these contributing factors:

- Your relationship with your child
- Their current work ethic level
- The company and external influences they have in their life
- Their daily schedule and other commitments
- The goals they have in racing
- Their observations of your work ethic

And the biggest influence of all when it comes to developing a career, comes down to how badly they want it.

If the passion and desire to become the world champion (or whatever big goal they have) is absent, then expecting them to work hard for it is nearly impossible.

If your child or children are not passionate – or more precisely if they are not obsessed with their racing – then getting them to increase their voluntary work rate will always be a challenge.

As you may have found in your own life, to grind your way forward in such a tough sport you need the emotional fuel to propel you forward each day. Without that, your child won't put in that extra hour of calls, they won't knock on that potential sponsor's door, they won't relentlessly study the onboard video footage and they will only go so far.

Let's be honest: how hard do we work on things we don't care much about?

Step 1 – Face the truth

If your son or daughter is to improve their work rate towards their racing, they need to get to the point where it is genuinely the first thing they think of when they open their eyes in the morning.

It must mean so much to them that they are compelled to take action. Pushing yourself to do the things you need to do is much harder than being pulled towards your goals. They need to be fully attracted to what they want in this sport and be self-driven.

Ideally, they need to get to the point where they become addicted to the process and the chase so they feel energised by their pursuit.

I know this could be slightly controversial... but most of the time I see drivers not working hard enough, it is because their heart isn't really in it and racing is more of a passion for the parent/s than it is for their child.

This is very, very common. You see this all over the paddock: the parents are super-involved and proactive in their child's racing endeavours, but the young drivers themselves seem to just go along with it because it's fun to race and it keeps their parents happy. Or they keep going with it because they don't want to let their parents down.

In this situation, it is way too far-fetched for us to expect them to be inspired to work hard on their racing and for them to be self-motivated to do the 'not so fun' stuff.

We are tricking ourselves if we think a driver will step up for something they don't care enough about. It just won't happen.

I always want to be straight with you and tell you how things are. So before we get more into the work ethic aspects, first I want you to answer this question: ***How much does your child actually want this?***

The one thing I have noticed about the hardworking drivers is that they can't even breathe without having racing in their lives. It's quite literally all they think about – and because of this they only feel fulfilled if they have spent the day taking actions toward their racing goals.

We all know what it is like to be driven towards achieving something: it makes us feel alive and we don't even question spending 18 hours straight on our passion. Our desire for something is the fuel that produces work ethic.

So first off, let's address the elephant in the room and understand how much they actually want to race.

If this isn't something that you are struggling with, please skip the rest of this step. But if you are struggling, here are a few ways in which you could address this.

You could just ask them

Create the right time and setting when you are both engaged in the moment and mentally present, and softly ask them "If you could do anything with your life, what would you do? Who would you be? What would you be doing if you could wave a magic wand and live your perfect life?"

These open questions are far better than you getting annoyed with your child and asking them something like "do you even want to race?" They will always respond with a "yes" to that question because it's an automated response when questioned in that way.

Instead, I suggest trying to align yourself with them and have some philosophical chats over a certain time period. Get their mind to open up to what they really want in life.

Asking open-ended questions can take your conversation down many avenues as they navigate their way to letting you know what they actually care about in this world.

If it's not racing, that is completely fine and you can breathe a sigh of relief! Not only will you save yourself a lot of money, you can now let your child live a life that inspires them, setting them free to do something they genuinely care about.

If they don't have any other interests at the moment, that is fine too. Many of us get to our sixties and still don't know what we want out of life, but at least they can spend the next thirty years or so figuring it out and trying things.

We don't all need to be success-hungry workaholics striving to become champions in some sector. This is less about career success and more about starting the journey to the truth to understand what they actually want. Their desires must come first when we are talking about this topic.

When having these conversations, it is important that they don't feel judged for the answers they are giving you. If they do, they will just give short answers and simply say what you want to hear. That's no good to anyone long term.

So pick your moment and maybe have many different conversations with them to help them let their guard down and be truthful with you.

Like I mentioned in the previous chapter, a good time could be when you have both reached the top of the big hill after a long hike, and you have a nice philosophical moment together as you look out at the view.

OK I may have gone too far here and created a Hollywood moment but I think you get what I mean!

Watch and listen

This is where you can flex your body language and psychology muscles to take in what your child communicates to you.

Due to you knowing your own child/children better than anyone else on this planet, we can use that knowledge to your advantage.

My suggestion is to take the time over a month or so to absorb what your driver says and how they react to things that are related to racing.

If you watch the micro-movements in someone's body language, you can often get a read on what they are feeling at any given time. This is especially true in moments when they are compelled to give an instant reaction to something.

Over the years we have all preloaded and linked certain emotions to certain body postures and movements that we hold. This is great because it allows us to understand what others are feeling just by looking at the way they use their body. I want you to use this.

To give you a scenario where you will see this play out, let's say you inform your driver that there is a test day next week that you want them to go to. But when you tell them, you notice their shoulders drop by a few millimetres, then they let out a sigh as they tilt their head with an expressionless look on their face.

If your driver reacts this way, it's safe to say they are not motivated to go.

If your child did have this kind of reaction and you wanted to truly understand what they were feeling or thinking, then as weird as this sounds, you could stand or sit in front of a mirror and literally mimic the posture and overall body language your child was pulling.

In doing this you would create a similar emotion to what they were producing at that time and you would effectively be mind-reading them.

You will already be very good at reading other people's body language but I just want you to consciously notice the way your driver reacts to things. Then start to think about the emotional reactions they are having, and more importantly, why they are having them.

If they are not motivated to go to the track or work on their racing, then we must get to the bottom of things.

Also listen to their language. The words we use also communicate things from our internal world. It sounds obvious but I believe that virtually everything we say, the words we use and the way we say them, suggests something about us and how we mentally operate.

As a basic example, if you talk to someone who loves to feel significant in life and who loves to tell people of their achievements, you will often hear them say things like "When I achieved..." or "When I studied at Harvard..." or "I was once good friends with..." They will persistently spew out self-validating language to raise their public profile and fulfil their need to feel special.

If you hear someone doing this, you know their main inner need is significance. They must feel and communicate why they are worthy of being loved or respected. They are not necessarily big-headed and they may not even realise they sound like they are boasting, but this is a classic case of them allowing their internal goals to seep through to their external world verbally.

This comes out even more in a public setting, like at a party. Their insecurities are flaring up in that environment so you will notice their language follows a more boasting-based script. They will do this even more in a situation where they are made to feel insignificant and they want to prove to others that they are worthy.

This is being very stereotypical, but the point I am making is that we can also use this to mind-read and get a feel for your child's feelings.

You may well be doing these things already, but if you are not and you want to be more of a silent investigator to observe what racing means to your child, these tips can help you.

All in all, for this first step we just want to understand how much your child actually wants this. To do this you have to put your own wishes to one side for a while in order to hear what your child is really after – and if racing means enough to them.

If you come to the conclusion that their desire for racing is absent, then it's time to have a calm and open conversation with them to explore what they actually want to do in life. They can always come back to racing if they change their mind further down the road, but it's a losing battle to expect them to have a good work ethic when their heart isn't in the game.

That's why this step is called 'face the truth'.

However, if they have convinced you that racing means everything to them and they give you a clear indication that they are prepared to do anything to become a champion, including working harder, then move on to Step 2.

Step 2 – Motivation

Motivation is a widely misunderstood term but in this context I am referring to motivation as the feeling that someone feels when they are compelled to take action towards something that they care about.

Motivation is the mindset we have when we have an abundance of mental energy and we point it directly towards making progress. It's actually more than just in the mind: if you are seriously motivated to do something then you physically feel it in the centre of your chest and elsewhere in your body.

Even the facial expressions of a motivated person are easy to see; you can always spot when someone has hunger in their eyes.

If we are to get your driver working as they should be, we need to get them firing on all cylinders mentally and help them create the very emotions that will inspire them to get a move on.

Following your discussion with them in Step 1 (when they convinced you they deeply love racing) you can strike while the iron is hot and get them to explain more about their ambitions in the sport. This is obviously to ensure that you keep fuelling that emotional fire.

Once you get someone in an inspired state of mind, you can delve into their mind more to find out what their motivations are – by quickly asking them something like "What is it about racing that you love so much?" or "Why do you want to race?"

The answers your driver gives you will allow you to fully understand what motivates them now, and this will give you the information you need to help motivate them in the future.

To take this a step further, you could even get them to use their imagination and picture what things will look like when they succeed. You can get them to describe their future Victory Scene, which will be the moment when they lift that trophy or reach their dream.

When this is done well, helping your driver explain and virtually see what they most desire, so they can mentally step into that Victory Scene, it can be a seriously powerful way to motivate someone.

If your driver has a dream, make it your mission to help them breathe life into that dream as often as you can. Keep that fire burning.

Young children are great at using their imagination, so they will find this very easy to do. You just might have to work a little harder with the older drivers.

Being the person who knows your child better than anyone else, you are the perfect person to do this. Even if it isn't fitting with the relationship you have had with them up to this point, now might be the time to change that and start to open up the heart of the person you love most in this world.

A parent is there to show us the way and teach us how to thrive and survive in life, but a parent should also be the person who helps us be all we can be. By doing some of the things I have mentioned here you will be doing just that.

Step 2 may be a short step but it's an effective one. We must never underestimate the power of a person who has a clear vision for what they most desire and the energy to go get it. It's the very foundation for building a strong work ethic.

Step 3 – Have a system in place

Once they are bouncing off the walls with enthusiasm (or mildly excited) we need to channel that mental energy towards making a clear plan of attack.

When I say 'plan of attack' I mean we need to show them the very steps they must take, in order to get what they want. If you get someone fired up to take action, it's important to immediately show them what they can do to progress things.

In my own life I sometimes like to use my Computer Game Theory when planning an assault on my career. That's where

I gamify the whole process and literally see myself and the situation as if I am the character in a game.

Just like with any third-person computer game like Grand Theft Auto or Fortnite, you have the following structure in place:

1. You know what your North Star Goal is; the ultimate goal you have in life.
2. You then reverse engineer that main goal into levels that act as stepping stones that will take you closer to it. I like to call these levels 'quests'.
3. Then each quest will have individual 'missions' within it that all need to be completed.

So the goal is the compass that guides you and the mission/quests are the building blocks you will use to build your future.

As you can tell, I see things in a childish way... but I really benefit from gamifying my life to make things simple and help me remain resourceful. It is a strange mental technique but it is something that young drivers really buy into.

They love taking the seriousness out of daily life and treating the whole thing like a game. They understand there are serious repercussions for certain actions but usually they enjoy playing what is the most difficult and realistic game of all... life.

Their North Star

To start creating a plan I suggest sitting down with your child and getting them to explain what their dream goal is. This is the huge goal, the one they are a bit embarrassed even to say in public because they know people will laugh at them.

This is not setting your child up to fail, this is just setting the dream ending of their game so we can accurately set their internal compass – and for them to understand the amount of commitment it will take.

It is irrelevant whether they achieve their main goal or not; the goal isn't always possible to achieve. Instead the purpose of the goal is to drive them forward and to help them make the right decisions. Oh... and of course, to help raise our work ethic.

If we have a huge outlandish goal, and we have a plan for how to get it, we cannot help but feel compelled to take action each day. So we need to help create this in your child's life.

Once they have described and written down what they would love to achieve in the next ten or twenty years, then we move on to mapping it out.

Set the quests

Next we need to identify the three or four things he or she must accomplish in the next year if they are to stay on track with their North Star.

To give you an example, if a 16-year-old driver claims their North Star is to become an F1 World Champion, their main quests over the next 12 months may be:

- To win or at least stand out in the F4 championship
- To raise enough sponsorship to pay for F3
- To get signed up by an F1 junior programme

These are very clear and solid quests this driver can focus on and spend all their time attempting to achieve.

Things don't come bigger than a driver shooting for F1, and when someone has a huge goal like that you will notice their quests (what they want to achieve in the next year) are also quite large.

The bigger the goal, the bigger the steps.

When setting the quests that your driver will embark on over the next 12 months, I suggest that the quests must be 'stretch goals'. The kind of medium to short term goals that will seriously push them, but are possible to achieve if all goes well and they pull out all the stops.

So no wishful thinking here, just very clear goals that will stretch them and force them to work their tail off.

Set the missions

Once you are both happy with the main quests, we then move onto the individual missions that will help them achieve them. Missions are the smaller, more immediate goals.

The driver will start each week by looking at their three or four main quests and ask themselves: "What could I possibly do, this week, that will leap me forwards towards my quests?"

By doing this each Monday or Sunday night, they are creating a To Do List that gives them obvious steps to take over the coming week.

It may look something like this:

Quest - To win the F4 championship

This week's missions for this quest:

1. *Go to the team for a full day of prep and sim work*
2. *Do four days at the gym working on my updated program*
3. *Review the previous race to highlight what I need to improve*
4. *Do the online sim training with my coach and work on those things*
5. *Read 50 pages of the engineering book my engineer gave me*

6. *Look for track days at the next circuit we go to*
7. *Sign up for the car control day*

This is the kind of thing they will do for each main quest to make sure they fill the week with actions that force them forward. If they are serious about their racing, they will have very little white space left on their calendar.

They should then spend the week executing and adjusting the missions. When they get to the end of the week, they must then look back on what they have done and whether or not they have passed their missions.

Basically that means they will have either completed their daily tasks or have not.

You can join them doing this if they want to be held accountable. Each Sunday you could sit down together to see how well they performed that week, then design the next week.

If they constantly rinse and repeat this process, and keep themselves motivated, after six months or so you can both monitor things and see if things need adjusting or modifying in some way.

Use Software

When I do this for myself and for my drivers I use my own designed Excel document that helps us organise things and forces us to progress. To gamify things further you can even give them a score for their work rate or other aspects of their performance over the week. Alternatively they can score themselves.

The aim is for your child to get addicted to taking the required actions that will help them get what they want in racing. This puts a system in place that helps them monitor progress and lets them know they are doing things that are making an impact.

When on a long journey, you obviously need the motivation and to have a plan in place, but you also need to know whether you are going the right way or not. Using software like Excel or Google Drive Sheets can help you do that.

Your driver may get lazy from time to time but if they are determined to succeed and to give all this a go, this will help get them back on track after a few lazy weeks.

If you go to my website theracedrivercoach.com (on the downloads page) then you will see an Excel document by the name of 'Maxi Attack Form'. That is the basic version of what I use and it will give you a good template for organising the weekly tasks your driver must do.

Take a look and make it your own.

Step 4 – Keep the energy high

Remember that when you are doing this with a younger driver, you must keep the positive emotions going and help them attach those emotions to the missions they have set for themselves.

Maybe they could get some kind of prize or have some ritual in place that rewards them for accomplishing all of their missions in a week.

I may repeat this a few times in this book but as humans we are addicted to progress, so your child must see that all of these actions are actually advancing things.

If you keep spirits high and focus forward, they will more likely improve their work ethic. Over time, their newly found dedication will become more of a habit. Long term we want them to automatically put the work in, but in the beginning we may need to use motivational tactics to keep igniting their fire and their focus.

Step 5 – Help them with the hurdles

Your driver will have certain missions that are daunting to them, so they will be tempted to put those particular tasks off for another day if they aren't wearing their brave pants.

They may have started the week with courage and optimism (when writing out that week's missions) but then when it comes to actually executing that mission, they may wimp out.

Missions that cause drivers to procrastinate due to fear are normally the ones that include things like cold-calling a sponsor or having an awkward conversation with someone in the team. Whatever missions they are, I urge you to notice when this happens and question them about it at the end of the week.

It may just be a case of you giving them a nudge or a motivational speech, or there could be more to it. Either way, make sure you cover it when discussing how their week went.

That's another reason why I like to gamify it by self-scoring things like the driver's work rate. You could get them to score themselves out of ten on how well they executed, on how disciplined they were, how many days they completed all their tasks or even how brave they were that week.

All these things can be scored and your driver can understand whether their work ethic was up to scratch that week. Making it a game and something that is monitored in this way will hold them accountable and make the whole process of working hard that bit more interesting.

It's important that your driver understands the most daunting missions are usually the ones that bring the most rewards if they go well. Failure, being rejected or even public embarrassment is likely, but the upside is worth it.

Your driver might just need a hand expanding their comfort zone, but once they do it a few times things will get easier. Sometimes they need to be reminded of this... don't we all?

Step 6 – Do not do too much for them

Remember this is all to help them make their own way and improve their work ethic. If they make a pathetic attempt at creating or executing their missions, please refrain from doing it for them.

When parents step in on tasks that race drivers should be doing, they quickly take their foot off the gas and suffer from learned laziness. They need to understand that if the job needs to get done, they are the ones who need to do it.

Tough love is a necessity when teaching someone work ethic and discipline. Just watch a series of *SAS: Who Dares Wins* and see how well it works.

OK, you don't have to scream and shout expletives to your driver every waking minute... but when you are trying to carve a driver, you need to chisel off some big chunks first.

Accountability is one important ingredient for success so we need to help them realise this so they can take the lead. They need to fully digest the fact that if they don't put in the work, their missions don't get done.

They need to be the boss when it comes to their career.

The ultimatum

If – after all this work you have put in to help them improve their work ethic and commitment – they still fail to wake up and raise their standards, this is the point that I would hit them with reality.

If I was paying for their racing and they still couldn't be bothered to fully commit themselves, I would immediately pull the money. I would flat out refuse to fund their racing if they can't even meet me halfway. If I did, it is literally throwing money away.

It's disgraceful that there are drivers on our grids who happily let their parents pay for their racing, letting them run around like headless chickens as they try and juggle their jobs while organising the driver's own lazy ass.

It kills me to see this and as a coach I won't stand for it. It's downright rude and all I can think of is my younger self who had to bleed in order to earn the money to race when I was a teenager.

So be strong here. If they remain lazy, give them an ultimatum and stick to it.

This isn't conditional love; this is conditional funding.

They need to constantly prove that they can carry this career for themselves and they need to be self-made.

If you watch a fly-on-the-wall documentary or autobiography of any true sporting champion, you don't see their parent's pleading with them to go to the gym or to give a shit about their career. All real champions are self-driven and their hunger drives them to action. It's all they can think about.

You can't fake this. If your driver starts to get the reputation in the paddock for not being a hard worker, their career is done. That's a seriously harmful reputation to have and people will never be inclined to give them an opportunity.

Teams will happily take the money from a lazy driver but they won't give them a helping hand when it comes to their career. Not for long anyway.

That's it

A mix of these strategies has worked well for me throughout my time coaching drivers and I think some of them may help you with your driver.

There may be a lot of information in this chapter that doesn't fit your situation, but I have given you a broad view of things so I can touch upon at least one thing that will help you and your driver.

As with every other subject in this book, I am just giving you ideas and frameworks. You can modify what I say to create what works for you.

Make it your own.

CHAPTER 8

TAKING TOO LONG TO IMPROVE

Things don't stand still for very long in the fast-paced world of motorsport. The cars are being innovated, the circuits are being upgraded and the teams work tirelessly to make themselves and their cars more competitive.

This sport demands progress and if you don't consistently keep moving forward, you will soon find yourself in career quicksand.

Yet when it comes to the actual race drivers, we find many of them are effectively treading water when it comes to their personal progress.

Every single race driver has their individual flaws – which is normal for any competitor due to them being human – but what we see is that many drivers fail to improve their flaws over time so they constantly come up against the same personal performance blocker year after year.

It is common to see drivers who suffer from certain shortcomings in their early years of racing and they still have those same traits decades later.

For example, they may be the kind of driver who emotionally flies off the handle when things are not going their way, or they mentally crumble when the pressure is really on. You see them do it when they are racing karts, then you witness them repeat the same behaviour when they are racing in cars in their thirties.

They may have stepped up a few categories in this timeframe but they are still making the same mistakes and they haven't really progressed as a driver or as a competitor. Not mentally anyway.

If lack of progress is something you are facing with your driver right now, and they are not making the gains you think they should be, in this chapter I will give you some pointers to help you structure their training so you can help them move forward.

Use your frustration

You know all too well that children progress at various speeds and learn in their own way. Race drivers and adults are no different.

Some drivers take to driving like a duck to water and are up to speed in no time, others take a lot longer. I have had some drivers who are ready to win in cars with only a handful of initial test days, and by contrast I have had drivers who have needed 70 days of testing before they are able to even get into the top 15.

We all mature at different ages; some of us get things quickly while others take more time to digest things.

It can be very frustrating when your driver takes longer to master the craft of driving (and the other important qualities) because they will be told the same thing over and over again for months on end, yet they keep making the same errors or fail to make the changes everyone expected from them.

It is easy for us to worry about the cost of a driver who is slow at progressing. We worry about the money being spent, the time being lost on the basics and how far off their teammates they are.

Many parents also worry about how this looks from the outside. They get embarrassed to tell others how many actual test days their child has done. They view it as an unfair advantage or a bad thing.

In any other sport, the more training an athlete has done the better, but in our ego-driven sport people like to create the image that their driver is a born natural and hasn't done much testing compared to the other drivers. I know it's pathetic, but people often take this viewpoint.

Parents often have high expectations of their children and they wonder why their child cannot do what other drivers are doing out there. This is followed by the parents, coaches and/or engineers becoming frustrated with the driver, which is where things can quickly take a downward spiral.

If this is your situation, I suggest we should not take that path. Do not let your frustration hamper their performance further and cause friction in the parent/child relationship. Instead, I urge you to use the energy your frustration creates within you, and turn it into motivation to help them.

To do this we need to look at things through your driver's eyes – because for them it is even worse. They too feel the frustration that you have and they also become disheartened by it all, but on top of that they also have the embarrassment in front of their team or the other drivers because they cannot do what others are doing so easily.

Always remember that all they care about is making you proud. So if you start to show that you are disappointed in them and that their performance is causing you to think less of them, they will either lose interest or their mojo.

They are competing as best as they can in the big ugly sport of motorsport where adults are shouting, parents are competing against each other through their children and everyone is in it for themselves. So do not be yet another enemy or somebody attacking your child just because they still haven't got their brake shape quite right yet.

Again, you will naturally get frustrated and you will be pulling your hair out at times... but let's be bigger than our negative emotions and use them to fuel our motivation to find out how we can help the driver.

See it as code breaking

Each time I take on a driver who has been struggling with a certain aspect of their driving or their personal performance for a long time, I like to view it as a challenge. I take it on as something that can be solved or something that we can at least come up with a solution for.

I will try and explain things differently to them; I will introduce different types of training and I will constantly brainstorm ways in which I can help the penny drop.

There will be an unlock for them (a time when things start to click) and when this is aligned with the correct mindset and confidence levels, they suddenly take off and reach at least a good standard.

I'm not saying every driver has the ability to drive as well as a Lewis Hamilton or a Max Verstappen, because these drivers don't come along very often. But we can at least get any driver to improve and help them perform at their best. That's the first port of call here – and who knows how good they will eventually become?

Attempting to unlock the next level of performance from a driver can be seen in a similar way to how a bank robber would look at a safe or a vault. The bank robber knows the vault door is locked so they employ their best safecracker to get to work on cracking the combination lock code.

The safecracker will patiently and relentlessly turn the dial on the lock while listening for any mechanical movement within it. The small noises that come from the lock's internals are subtle hints for what the code is. The safecracker will follow these hints and stick to the process until they either unlock that vault door or until time's up and the police are on their back.

I see drivers' problems in a similar way to this. They will be struggling with a certain aspect of their performance, and I put it upon myself to help them seek the answers they need. I also get hints to the answers I seek by listening to how they speak, how they react to things and how they mentally process the external world.

Like the safecracker, I must also remain patient, I must be relentless and I must not give up.

So far this approach has worked well for me, and I would love for you to take a similar approach when it comes to your driver.

All your driver really cares about is making you proud. They are just as frustrated as you, just as disheartened – and maybe it is even worse for them because they may feel embarrassed that they haven't made the progress they maybe should have by now.

Don't get me wrong: at times I find myself pulling my hair out because a driver is just not getting it but when I find myself in those situations I have to remind myself that this really is a game and the answer is there somewhere.

There is always a solution.

The solution

It goes without saying that your driver's race team will be doing what they can to help your driver improve. If they have an engineer or mechanic running them, that individual should be coming up with ways which they think will help.

That's all good but it's the driver who should be taking on most of the responsibility. They must be motivated to move things forward and they must make it their mission to improve. Once that is in place, things should be approached in a structured way.

To give you some kind of coaching blueprint and show you what I do with drivers, here are the steps that I take a driver through when they want to improve their results.

1. Do a full performance assessment
2. Build a bespoke training plan
3. Score and feedback following event
4. Review the feedback and adjust the training/strategy accordingly
5. Repeat Steps 3 and 4 until the driver improves

Simple, right?

Self-development and the structure behind it is always simple. It's within each step where the magic happens.

Just so you know, I like to document things first before actually working on the challenges drivers have. The first two steps mentioned here are where I get things down on paper (Excel documents) to get the driver's strengths and weaknesses out in the open so we can begin to plan how we will tackle their challenges.

This way you also have a paper trail so you can monitor their progress and put in the training or strategies to help them improve the things hampering their performance.

To explain things better, here are the steps in more detail.

Step 1 - Do a full performance assessment

Even though a driver may be coming to me with a specific challenge, I like to do a full performance assessment anyway, so I can understand the big picture and learn more about the driver globally.

This assessment is where we sit down either in person or via a video call to talk about all the aspects related to their performance and their career.

We will first establish what their long and short term goals are in racing. For now, I stay away from their current problem and make sure their mind is thinking about what they want in racing.

Then I get clear on what their current situation is by asking where they are racing and what results they have achieved up to now.

Once this part is done, we can see the path they must walk and start to talk about areas they must excel in if they are to successfully walk that path. This is all recorded on my coaching software and pretty much cast in stone so we can always refer back to our initial conversation.

Put things into boxes

After this initial goal-setting stage, we then turn our attention to their overall performance.

It is part of my coaching philosophy to compartmentalise things. So when I am working with a driver I like to take certain components that contribute to and influence their overall performance and split them into their own sections – or boxes, as I like to call them.

Typically, I will use the following boxes:

- Box 1 - Mental Performance

- Box 2 - Driving
- Box 3 - Team/Car Performance
- Box 4 - Work Ethic
- Box 5 - Environment (lifestyle)
- Box 6 - Fitness

For me these are the main areas that a driver needs to perform well in if they are to create a career or achieve their racing goals. Some drivers may require more boxes – like Sponsorship & Business Skills or Leadership Skills if they are solely in charge of getting the racing funds in place – but these are the most common ones.

By the way, this can be applied to anyone – no matter what sport or job role they wish to improve their performance in. The boxes will just obviously have different titles if a CEO is using this for their own performance at work.

We then go deeper into the assessment by grading the driver in all the elements within each box. These are the subcategories for each area; for example, the Mental Performance box will have these elements within it:

- Achieving my optimal mindset throughout qualifying
- Current confidence levels whilst in the car
- Handling distracting thoughts
- Emotional control in races
- Regaining my focus following a mistake or when under pressure

The Driving box has elements like:

- Braking
- Driving in slow speed corners
- Starts
- Consistency
- Overtaking

- First lap performance

Each box typically has between 10 to 50 different elements that we will speak about and that the driver will score themselves on.

If we were going through their Driving box then when it comes to scoring themselves, I will ask them something like: "Out of 10, how good is your braking in this car and why?"

They will score their current braking performance and give me an explanation for that score. Maybe they'll say: "My braking is about 3 out of 10, because I cannot seem to consistently hit the required peak. This is causing me to lock up whilst entering the corners that need hard braking."

If this was the case, they would most likely also score their slow corner performance low because those are the corners that require a good brake shape.

As the driver scores each element of each box, you begin to paint a picture of what kind of driver you have in front of you. This allows you to prioritise what needs working on, while you also learn what their strengths are.

Once you have done this with their Mental box and the Driving box you start to see patterns that help expose the cause of their issues. The code breaking has begun and they are giving you the hints you need either to investigate further, or to think of ways the driver can work on these areas.

Either way, when doing this you really understand clarity is power, and the driver also feels this.

Most of the time I only do the first three boxes initially (Mental, Driving and Team/Car) with a driver unless we need to go further and it becomes clear that their fitness or work ethic needs improving.

To start, all the scores given by the driver and the comments we note next to each element are totally subjective. It is how the driver views their own level, so it is important for them to be as honest as possible when doing this.

I also like to speak to someone else the driver is connected to, like their parents or their race team, to get another perspective so we can get an accurate account of things – just in case the driver has a skewed reality about where they are at.

The Mental box is also conversational. I get them to fill out a psychometric test and ask them to explain the so-called 'good and bad moments' they have had mentally whilst performing.

Once all this is done the driver can look at their scores as well as their goals and understand what needs to change if they are to even stand a chance at achieving their long term goal.

This is the point where they have a reality check or can plainly see things must improve. This creates motivation and ensures everyone is on the same page.

Progress is an important value we have as humans, so if this part is done correctly the driver will start to feel as if they are progressing just by exposing things in this way. It is a great step one for change and it will fire up their internal engine.

Step 2 - Build a bespoke training plan

Once you have done an overall assessment and singled out the main areas that need to be worked on – or other things that came out of it following your discussions with the driver – you have all the information you need to create a plan of attack.

Or to phrase it correctly, you can now design their training plan or development programme.

I do this by creating another document on Excel or Google Sheets. This one uses boxes too, but this time the only elements in each box are the areas your driver needs to improve or revolutionise. It is like having separate boxes with all their weaknesses within.

This is where you can use fewer boxes and only focus on what needs to be worked on. Then you will get the driver to grade them on a regular basis so we can monitor progress.

If you go to theracedrivercoach.com website, the Downloads page has a form from the *Get The Drive* book called the Maxi Attack Form. If you download it, you can see how I have done this with various areas. Feel free to use that form and make it your own by designing it however you want.

On that Excel document you will see each tab along the bottom is for a different area I want drivers to work on. Basically each tab is a different box.

If your driver only has to improve on their driving and their mental side, you only need those two boxes/tabs.

Depending on what they want to work on, a driver's boxes may only consist of a handful of different elements, like the following:

Mental Performance Box

- Emotional state at the beginning of a race
- My fear of crashing the car
- Regaining rhythm following a mistake
- Dealing with drivers in my mirror

Driving Box

- Race starts
- High speed corners
- Overtaking

If these are the only things they need to improve, so be it. You will now know where all your focus needs to go and you can begin to brainstorm ways to help them improve these areas.

Maybe the team can help design their test days to work on these things, maybe you need to employ a coach or maybe you can come up with leftfield ways to help them improve.

Either way, it's important that from now on, every time they work on their career or hit the track, they must intentionally aim to improve these areas. They do drills, exercises and sessions where these become a priority and everyone's efforts are aligned.

When you have this amount of clarity, unified motivation with all the people involved and you constantly try different ways to improve them, you will be surprised at how quickly your driver can turn things around.

Step 3 - Score and feedback following each event

Now that we have a list of priorities in each area (box) and we have come up with a plan for how to improve each, you can use that form or a similar one to keep track of progress.

Simply sit down with the driver after each test and race event and go through the boxes by scoring and discussing each of them. You guessed it: you can create another Excel or Sheets document for this where you have a different tab for each event.

Each sheet has their boxes of priorities on it, and next to each element you have a drop down score and a comments section next to that.

You can use this to record things and see if the training strategy worked on that particular outing.

If you are seeing them improve in certain areas, you can keep that training. But if over a certain period of time you notice that they are still not improving in certain areas, it may be time to change your approach and try something else to help them.

I do this with all my drivers and it massively helps them move forward. They know that when we have a session following an event, they will come armed with their scores, we will delve into how things went and what we need to do next time.

Once they turn some of their weaknesses into strengths, we take them off the list and replace them with another element of their performance they want to improve to reach the next level.

This becomes a never-ending pursuit for excellence.

The reason I score things isn't just to get a gauge with where they are at; it is my way of gamifying things. I like to see my drivers as if they are players on the FIFA football videogame. Each player has scores next to each attribute or skill, like dribbling, running speed, shooting, tackling etc.

It is my aim to have this for each driver I work with. Again, most of the scores are subjective. But it still allows us to help them improve as a driver and as a person.

Step 4 - Review the feedback and adjust

This step is basically where you rinse and repeat.

They go on track to compete or test with certain performance-related objectives in mind. They sit down after the event to score and review their boxes, and you both decide whether to keep doing what you are doing or to change things. Then you go again.

This process is done over and over until the driver improves the areas that they are not happy about or the ones holding them back.

That's it

In essence, this is how I approach helping drivers. Obviously the magic happens in the training and techniques that you teach a driver, but if you have knowledgeable people around you in the team or if you have a good coach, that aspect is taken care of.

All in all, the best way to help a driver improve is to get very clear on what needs to improve: to unearth just how much these things are holding your driver back, then to come up with ways for improving it and to monitor all the progress.

It is like an experiment where you know what you want to achieve and you record your finding as you experiment with things.

Coaching and helping your driver improve is a very simple process, but you must do it in a structured way if you are to help them advance.

CHAPTER 9
CAN'T QUALIFY WELL ENOUGH

During a race weekend, you will often see drivers who can lay down competitive lap times in testing but when it comes to the all-important qualifying session, they underperform and don't produce the results they are capable of.

There can be a number of reasons for this. They may...

... make too many mistakes

... not fully understand how to use new tyres

... tend to overdrive in qualifying

... tend to underdrive in qualifying

... not adjust to the change in track conditions

... often get caught up in traffic

These are just six of the common external reasons why drivers underperform in qualifying, and they are the kind of things that will hurt a driver's career over time.

A driver's ability to drive well when the chips are down is the 'sporting' side of motorsport. This is where we get into human performance – and, as with other sports, the competitors who win are the ones who can consistently deliver when it matters.

If your driver is struggling with this during a season, I want you to see this as yet another opportunity because, believe it or not, it won't be just your driver who is struggling in this area. Many of the grid will have the same problem.

You will notice your driver doing this more, but that's only because you are watching them closer than the other drivers. This is great news because it means that if we can sort this aspect out, your child will leapfrog a handful of drivers in qualifying before the racing has even begun.

So it's important to approach this challenge, like all challenges, with optimism and positive energy. If so you are going to help your driver become better in a vital area that, if done correctly, will be a game-changer for them.

I say this because when you are working on aspects of your 'game' that are non-negotiables when it comes to performing, to approach your training with a sense of worry or negative mental energy causes too much frustration and doesn't allow the mind to operate freely.

When training your driver, they are far better off being in a curious state of mind where they are hungry to put the work in and they fully understand what an opportunity this is. It's exciting to be working on this stuff due to the ability it can give them. By doing this, they will open up and allow themselves to perform at their current best. That's all we can ask.

So have no judgement here, no negative atmosphere, just straight-up training where everyone present is working together and globally moving forward.

This is a very important but rare approach.

The Five-Step Coaching Process

When a driver comes to me to improve their qualifying, I initiate a straightforward coaching framework that helps us discover what is really going on and how best to help them.

To simplify things, here is the five-step process I take people through.

1. **Identify the external issue.** First I will listen to their version of what is going on. They will say something like what we mentioned at the beginning of this chapter (the effect).
2. **Ensure the driver is motivated.** The driver must be very determined to improve this area.
3. **Get to the core reason.** Identify what the real cause is.
4. **Come up with a way to improve the core reason.** Get the training in place that helps them improve the real cause so they can perform better in qualifying.
5. **Monitor and measure the progress.** Have a system in place that allows us to rate the progress. If no progress is made, we adjust training and come at things from a different angle until we get it right and the driver improves.

This is a coaching structure that can be used for most things you want to improve. It may seem obvious but the basis for self-development often is.

How this looks

To run you through how this works, let's take a look at a fictitious driver called Rob.

Rob is aware that he is not delivering in qualifying. He has seen it for himself and other people have started to notice it, so he fully understands it is an issue he must address. He comes to me for help, so I take him through the Five-Step Coaching Process to help him fix his qualifying woes.

He starts off by telling me what he is doing in qualifying and why he is not getting the results that he is capable of.

He will say something like: "I keep over-pushing and making mistakes when the tyre is at its best."

Once he has told me everything from his point of view and he is clear about what he needs to fix, we move onto Step 2. This will be my attempt to get him motivated to improve.

He will already be partially motivated to even call me in the first place... but I need to get him to the point where he is seriously determined to sort this out; where it becomes his sole priority and he is revved up to change things.

To do this we use the Pain & Pleasure Principle to see how things play out if a) he continues to underperform in qualifying and on the flip side if b) he turns things round and executes as he wants in qualifying.

Creating two separate destinies

This is like creating two separate life journeys where we take a look at how his racing life will end up due to the actions he takes going forward.

Using his imagination, I will ask him: "What will your racing career look like in one year's time if you continue to screw things up in qualifying?"

I will get him to picture it, to explain it and to feel what it will be like.

He will tell me that his team will drop him, his sponsors will lose faith until he could possibly lose them, he will be disappointed in himself, he will be embarrassed, he will get told off by his father, etc, etc.

Once he has created this possible future and we have recorded it, I will then ask him to explain what things will be like, worst case scenario, if he continues to underperform in qualifying in two years. After that I get him to explain what things will be like in five years.

Now we have a bleak picture of what his racing career and life will look like if he carries on like he is. We make it as distasteful as possible and then deliver the killer blow by telling him: "Rob, this may all sound horrific but guess what? You are actually walking that path right now."

It may sound devastating but as things are, you are more likely to end up this way than not.

I really want him to face the reality of what this sport does to people when they are not performing and hit home some hard truths.

All of this is communicated to him in a caring way so he fully opens up yet doesn't feel judged. We are just working together to see things for how they really are.

Once I feel that he has fully embraced this and he has attached genuine pain to what could happen, it's time to give him an alternative future and paint out the path he will take if he does actually improve in qualifying.

This is where we create the pleasure aspect and do the complete opposite by asking him to explain what his racing will be like if he performs at his best in qualifying.

He will run me through that scenario and describe how his career could look in the future. He would then paint that picture in his mind and explain it.

Just as before I would then get him to tell me what his racing career and his life would be like in two years if he carried on performing well in qualifying. Finally we would take a sneak peek at his position in five years.

After we've done this, we have two very different timelines. One of them links pain to the vision of him failing; the other may see him getting picked up by an F1 junior programme or becoming a professional race driver.

All of this produces what we call 'motivation', which will increase his chances to put the necessary work in to turn things around.

Even though this is only Step 2 of the process, for many of the drivers I worked with this was already all they needed to get things sorted. The motivation alone can give them the emotional fuel needed to urge them to work harder and sort things out.

The Boxes

Once the driver is raring to go we can move into Step 3 and get to the root cause of their struggles in qualifying. This is where I like to compartmentalise things and put them into boxes.

This is my way of separating the main areas that could be responsible for a driver's qualifying challenges. On this occasion we could have three boxes for Rob, which would be:

Box 1 – His mental performance

Box 2 – His knowledge

Box 3 – His skillset

By doing this we can separate things to help us understand whether it's his mindset, his actual skills or his lack of knowledge that is responsible for his recent qualifying results.

This allows us to make the whole coaching process less overwhelming and make it easier for Rob to self-analyse.

I will literally draw these three boxes on a piece of paper and ask Rob to explain and factor in each area that could be hampering his performance in qualifying.

Box 1 – Mental performance

In this box we will discuss mental aspects that could be responsible. For example, if Rob tells me he overdrives and makes mistakes in qualifying, we need to dig deeper and understand why.

We need to get clear on what is driving the decision to push the car or kart too hard.

He may well respond by saying "I worry that I won't be fast enough" or "I am too focused on the lap time and it bullies me mentally."

When this is the case, we need to show his mind these fears and distractions are hurting things and they are actually creating the very thing he is fearing in the first place.

Performing with fear can often be a self-fulfilling prophecy. You fear not being 'good enough', so you tense up when competing and act in a way that stops you being 'good enough'.

The mind is a wonderful thing.

Our goal with Box 1 is to create clarity and help the driver understand their own psychology (mental habits) so they can decide if mental performance is a contributing factor.

Once we have gone through this area, whether we have unearthed something or not, it's time to move on to Box 2.

Box 2 – Knowledge

This is where we talk about the racing intelligence of the driver.

In this box we want to explore any part of the driving that the driver is not sure about. Is there something they don't fully understand that could be the reason for their qualifying performance?

For example, Rob may be able to do a competitive lap time on used tyres. But after talking about things he is not sure about (knowledge), he could admit he actually doesn't know how to warm the new tyres up correctly and doesn't fully understand the driving technique he needs on new tyres.

This means Rob is simply going out there in qualifying and probably expecting the new tyres to help him brake super-late. In fact the new tyres don't allow you to brake later, but they do help you enter the corner quicker and have better traction.

Not realising this, Rob would simply brake too late and then not even find out about the other parts of the corner because he has already overcooked things on the way in.

Here we have a simple case of the driver not understanding the fundamentals. This happens a lot.

Other things that drivers might not know are:

1. The most important part of each corner (perhaps corner exits for T1, T5 and T8 are crucial)
2. How best to use the tow from the car in front
3. How to position themselves better in traffic
4. How to feel when the new tyres are in and ready
5. What to feel for if they need to ask for a set-up change in qualifying
6. The different set-up changes they can quickly make if needed
7. How to use the tools in the cockpit to help the car handle as they like
8. What lines to choose and how to drive when more rubber is down on the surface
9. The lines and technique to use in the wet (if they struggle with wet qualifying)

10. Going back to the mental side, they might not actually know how to focus or generate confidence

What we are doing here is unearthing all the things the driver may not fully know. From this they can create a list of things they will learn or ask the team about.

Top drivers all have a high level of racing intelligence. They understand the most important aspects that contribute to winning a race weekend. They spend time studying their craft – and even though some top drivers cannot articulate their knowledge, they fully understand how to get the best out of themselves, out of their driving and out of their car.

This box is here to help the driver understand just how much they know or need to know.

Box 3 – Skillset

Box 3 is where we discuss the parts of a driver's performance that come down to their actual skill.

We cannot ignore that there are times when a driver has the correct mindset and they know exactly what to do (knowledge) but because they haven't mastered the required driving technique, they fail to deliver.

To give you some examples, drivers might not be proficient enough in these areas:

- Car control
- Driving quickly with understeer
- Driving quickly with oversteer
- Driving quickly in wet or changeable conditions
- Driving high speed corners
- Driving combination corners
- Driving slow corners
- The correct braking technique

- Rotating the car on entry
- Dancing with the car when it's on the limit

And the list goes on.

Like with the other boxes, the driver needs to be very honest with themselves and take a look at what skills are often required in qualifying, and to conclude whether they need to improve these skills.

If they have teammates who are delivering in qualifying then that's perfect: we can use them as a point of reference.

We can analyse the teammate's data and video footage to understand what skills they may have that are helping them compared to our driver.

We need to get to the cold, hard facts in this box and be very clear on what skills are under par and need to be improved going forward.

Rob's journey So far

Now we have completed three of the steps, we can check in with our driver Rob to understand his findings so far.

Rob came to us because he is not happy with his qualifying results. He said he keeps overdriving and pushes too hard in qualifying.

Then, after building some serious motivation to change this situation, he filled out the boxes and found the following:

Rob's Mental Performance Box

- I watch and worry too much about the lap time
- I attach my self-worth and identity to my results
- I create too much pressure on myself to perform so I cannot create flow

- I hate looking slow in public
- I care too much about what people think
- I panic when things are not going to plan

Rob's Knowledge Box

- I don't know how to focus without thinking of lap time
- I don't know how to regain focus after a mistake
- I don't understand how to get the most from new tyres and the technique needed
- I need to go on track fully understanding the most important part of each corner, because I often forget. This will help prevent me over-pushing on the entries at certain corners.

Rob's Skillset Box

- I know how to control my emotions, but I haven't mastered doing it on track
- I simply need to drive the new tyres better
- I need to practise the tyre-warming procedure more
- I must improve my overall car control so I can adjust things if I go into corners a little too hot

From this valuable information that Rob has provided, we can now get to work.

Come up with a way to improve the core reason

This is where we enter Step 4 of the coaching process and come up with training that will help Rob improve the core reasons for his lacklustre qualifying results.

First we will take a look through his boxes and decide what we think are the main priorities: the aspects that will make the biggest and quickest impact on his performance if he was to improve or resolve them.

As a coach I like to start off with the mental performance of the driver, because I believe this is the foundation for everything we do. Our mind is responsible for our perspective and our decisions – and this influences our actions. So what better place to start?

For Rob we do some mental training that helps him overcome his fear about what others think. Via a series of drills and techniques we help him develop a mindset that releases the 'mental ballast' so he can perform with a free mind.

This will be a mixture of training on his own, on the sim, in general public and at the track.

We would also show him how to focus when driving, no matter what is happening around him.

Then when it comes to his shortcomings in the knowledge department, he could sit down with his engineer and coach to understand more about what the tyre needs and what to remember for each corner.

In the learning phase, if he has in-car radio, he can also be reminded and talked through these things during the session. Knowledge is often the easy part because somebody usually knows the answer we are looking for. We just need to ask and store that information.

Finally, when we come to helping Rob improve his skillset, we will pick the most important areas and train him both on track and on the sim. Or to get creative, if it was something like car control, we could send him to rally or shunt driving school (or similar) to get comfortable with a car that is moving around.

Not only do I find it fun to hear a driver's challenges and come up with a training programme that helps them improve in all areas, but the driver also enjoys it. If they open up and they are honest, they are just about to experience one of a human's most important needs: the need for progress.

As living creatures, we thrive when we are progressing and evolving. That forward movement in life, in sport, in business and in our relationships is what we crave.

Couple this with a driver's results getting better at the same time, and you have one happy driver on your hands.

Monitor and measure the progress

Once we have exposed the core challenges, once we have a motivated driver who wants to improve and once they are training the very things they have highlighted, all we need to do is monitor the training and make sure that progress is being sustained.

You do this by having regular performance reviews. With my online coaching clients, we do weekly or bi-weekly Zoom sessions and literally grade how they are performing in the main areas we think are responsible for their performance.

We use an Excel document to record and score everything so we can see if progress is being made and whether they are advancing. We also get feedback from the race team or engineer, who keep an eye on things for us.

This means nothing is missed – and if they hit a plateau we can adjust the training or try different approaches.

There you have it

The coaching process that I have just run you through is the framework for what I believe works best when helping a driver perform at a higher level.

It is very straightforward and if you adopt this for your child you can help them improve. This is not just about qualifying, this can be used for virtually anything they want to improve, inside and outside of racing.

It's all about being honest, getting to the core reason, having the motivation to put the work in and coming up with effective training that can be monitored.

Then over time you will see progression and move on to the next performance challenge.

This journey for self-excellence never stops.

CHAPTER 10
CONTROLLING EMOTIONS WHILST ON TRACK

One of the most important skills that a person can possess, especially when they are required to perform on demand, is the ability to control – or at least manage – their emotions.

It is no secret that our mentality and the mental mode that we operate with directly influences the way we perform and how we react to situations. That's why I endeavour to teach emotional fitness to drivers, because the way they operate internally affects them big time externally.

If a driver is to get the best from themselves, they absolutely must have the mental skills in place that allow them to access their desired state of mind when needed and help them intentionally jump from one emotion to another.

A driver not only has to be the driver of their vehicle; they must also learn how to drive their mind.

If your driver has the ability to drive to a good standard but they can't seem to execute in qualifying, or if they allow certain emotions to negatively affect their decisions on track, they will always have a performance ceiling that will only allow them to go so far.

This is yet another life skill that drivers have the opportunity to condition in this sport, so I really want to make this area a priority in this book and in my training.

Emotional mastery is a never-ending pursuit but when you have a good grasp on it, you experience a sense of mental freedom and you have more control over your life. I will go as far as to say this is the number one skill a human needs if you want to live a fulfilled life and create the reality you desire.

Due to this being yet another big area and it being very individual to each driver, I will attempt to cover as much as I can in this chapter but I urge you and your driver to research this further after reading this book.

What emotions look like in drivers

When we talk about emotions in drivers we could easily think we are referring to them becoming tearful or angry while they compete. But I want to show you their emotions are called upon virtually every moment of their days at the track.

We see them accessing or using their emotions:

- When they need to focus during debriefs
- When they deal with receiving criticism from their engineer on their driving
- When they have to be confident while they are being interviewed
- When they are creating their optimal mindset before going out on track
- When they have to motivate team members
- When they recall what the car was doing while they relay their feedback

- When they are dealing with pressure from a driver behind them in the race

In fact, it's endless.

A driver needs to create the mindset they require for many different situations – and emotions are the very building blocks for creating these mental states or the level of focus they require.

To be a leader, a driver must be able to keep their head while others around them lose theirs, or while others are being distracted by what is going on in the moment.

Every driver and every person will have moments when they lose it mentally – and unwanted emotions creep in – but it's about the ability to get their mind back in the game and aligned with what is expected from them at any given moment.

Focus and body

To jump straight into this, I want to first talk about how our emotions are heavily influenced by what we think about, and how we use our body. I'd actually go as far as saying this is our superpower as human beings.

You may recall me talking about reading your child's body language so you can gauge their response to things. I want to use a similar strategy again, but this time it's to help them produce emotions.

To give you the best examples, I want you to imagine there is someone in front of you right now, sitting on a chair, who is experiencing the emotions of depression and worry.

As you pretend to look at them in your mind's eye, I bet you can tell me the kind of things they are thinking (what they are focusing on) and what they are doing with their body, right?

Of course you can.

You can already guess they will be focusing on the things that they are not happy about: they may be repeating words like “Why me?”, “Life is unfair”, “I am not worthy” or “What am I going to do now?”

On the physiological side of things (their body) you will automatically know their head will be looking down slightly, they will have a sad expression on their face, their shoulders will be slumped and their breathing will be shallow.

if they hold this physiology and with those thoughts running through their mind for long enough (maybe only a few seconds) they will produce the emotions of depression and/or worry.

Just by taking a quick look at them and by hearing their thoughts, you know full well what emotional state that person is creating.

That’s the big word here: **creating**.

I have found – indeed it has become a messed-up belief of mine – that we are individually responsible for what emotions we feel.

I know we are told chemical imbalances can cause uncontrollable emotions, and I am not disputing that because those who are far more versed in neurology than I am tell us this. But when it comes to managing our emotions you will be shocked at just how much control we have.

When we use certain thoughts and hold our body in certain ways, we actually create specific emotions.

I like to see us as mental chefs where we can cook up various emotions using various mental and physiological ingredients.

To make this sound as simplistic as possible, if you genuinely think happy thoughts and you hold your body as a happy person would, you can't help but produce the emotion called happiness.

If you think of things, memories and people that you are deeply grateful for, and you hold your body in a way that a grateful person would, you literally produce feelings of gratitude.

Our mind is like a factory. We can get it to produce emotions – and even chemicals – that we either want or don't want.

Nobody really teaches us this stuff in the standard education system, but since I have studied psychological sciences and worked on myself, let alone with my clients, I have realised just how much control we can have over our emotions if we train in that area.

In fact, you are already an expert at this.

If you are the type of person who often gets angry in daily life, you will already have that emotion down. You will be a master of creating anger for the small daily things that happen.

You may react in an angry state to someone cutting you up on the road or queue-jumping, whereas other people in the very same situation may react calmly as it doesn't really cause a reaction from them.

The only difference between your reaction and the person with the calm reaction, is the way you both translated the whole episode.

You may have immediately thought things like "What a dick!" or "How can you be so stupid and disrespectful?" or "I want to show you my dissatisfaction."

Then with your body, you may put that angry look on your face, sit bolt upright in your driver's seat, tense your whole upper body... and boom: you have literally just produced the emotion known as anger.

Whereas the person who reacted calmly may have thought something like "Ah, well, they are probably in a rush" or "I've got more important things to think about today than that douche bag" or "Fair play, I did the same yesterday..."

Meanwhile their body posture, facial expression and muscle tension doesn't change much from what it was previously as they were listening to their classical music playlist.

With these thoughts and by using their body in this way, their mind won't produce the emotion called anger. Instead it will produce calm or stay with the emotion they were running beforehand.

Same situation, very different response from two people.

We see this a lot in life, right?

This goes to show it isn't what happens to us in life, it's how we translate things that differs.

Your mind is always watching you

I want you to pretend your mind is always looking upon you (even though your mind is you) and it is waiting for your signal, so it knows what emotion to produce and deliver for you.

If it sees you are thinking angry thoughts and using your body in the usual angry way, it will think to itself: "Oh, this person is trying to access their angry state. Here you go..."

Your mind will then oblige.

We may have habitual ways of producing emotions without even thinking about them so they seem automatic, but we can disrupt these and change them any time we want.

This isn't a shallow positive mental attitude technique; this is using our thoughts and our physiology to put our mind into the state we want it to be in.

Most of us are not used to consciously doing this with what we are born with, so we go through life on autopilot, not taking control of our mindset. Instead we are taught to change our mental state by using external things like alcohol, drugs, food, music, etc.

Not all these external ways are unhealthy and some can be very helpful. But all I want to remind you of here is that we are constantly changing our emotions, so we already have this skill down.

Now we just need to make sure we create the emotions we want when we want them; and we know what our ingredients are for doing that.

Mathematical equations for emotions

I view the creation of emotions as if they were mathematical equations. What you do with your focus plus what you do with your body, equals the emotion that you feel.

Here are some examples of what I mean here.

Fear - Let's say a driver is feeling the emotion known as fear when they are attempting to drive high speed corners quicker. They may well be processing things like this...

Their focus (what they are thinking about):

1. How close the wall is on the exit
2. How they had an accident in a high speed corner once
3. Another driver's crash they saw on YouTube
4. How they don't want to incur damage costs or injury

Their body:

1. Gripping the wheel tight
2. Not looking into the corner early enough
3. Their whole body is tense
4. They take a deep breath and then hold their breath on approach

With this mental perspective and with their body being operated in this way, they will create the emotion called fear or panic.

The mathematical equation they are using here is:

Focusing on the worst case scenario and consequences + a tense body = Fear

Let's compare that to another driver who is usually the quickest on the grid when it comes to high speed corners. They are super-confident in the faster sections of a track and they feel comfortable driving them.

They typically operate their mind and body like this...

Their focus:

1. I want to rotate the car more and get to full throttle earlier
2. I know most drivers are slow here, so I must take advantage
3. Let's see if I can go even quicker through here
4. I love the feeling of the car on the limit like this

Their body:

1. Light hands on the wheel
2. Assertive but smooth movements on entry to manipulate the car
3. Looking far ahead and through the corner
4. Alert yet relaxed muscles and calm breathing

By mixing all of these mental and physiological ingredients together, this driver will produce a mindset that is confident and focused. Their equation would be:

Focusing on the process and the opportunity + a relaxed body = Confidence

Obviously there is more to this because our perspectives are heavily influenced by our belief system and our personal experiences in life. But at the surface level this is what is going on mentally and physically.

Simplifying things down and using the mental mathematical equation helps us start this process.

Once you know how a driver is translating things and how they back things up with the way they operate their body, you can begin to understand things and help them get to the cause of their emotions.

Semi-master this yourself first

Before you start to help your driver improve their emotional intelligence, please take the time to train yourself in this way.

If you are at work and feeling overwhelmed by something, stop for a moment. Come away from the office or the situation you are in, and change your perspective of what is going on by asking yourself different questions or having a more positive outlook on it. Then energetically change your posture, your breathing, your facial expression and how you are holding your body.

Make sure these thoughts and your body are aligned with the emotion you actually want to create, then get back into the situation with a different mindset.

This could be where the old saying "shake yourself out of it" came from. It's amazing how some of the sayings we grew up with (and ignore) are often pretty damn useful, if not life-changing.

So if you were feeling nervous because you have to go into the boardroom for a big sales pitch – and you want to create the emotion known as confidence – you would translate the situation in your mind via your thoughts and dramatically shift your physiology so it would match a confident person.

You may think things like:

- This is not really a sales pitch, I'm going to go in there to listen to what this person wants and just see if our services are a good fit
- I am going to use this meeting to help improve my people skills
- No matter what the outcome, I am going to learn so much here
- I want to help the potential client achieve their dreams, not mine

Straightaway, when you see things in this manner, the brain is already starting to deliver a different emotion and you will feel more relaxed.

Then as you think your thoughts, with your body you would:

- Sit up in your chair
- Get your chin up
- Put a big smile on your face
- Puff your chest out slightly and have a spring in your step

Then you clap your hands together, say something like "Let's do this!" And away you go...

You will have communicated to your mind what you want, and it would then respond by delivering that emotion to you. Then you will at least enter that boardroom in a much more resourceful way, and feel better about going in.

This is just a simple example but you can do this with any emotion.

Again, I would like you to semi-master this area prior to teaching your driver how to do it. Teaching something that you can already do makes it a lot easier to teach others. Plus you will come up with your own version of what I have talked about here.

There is no point trying to teach your driver emotional control if they constantly see you flying off the handle at things. We need to walk the talk when helping drivers, otherwise they won't listen.

How to start this

A good way to start emotional control training with your driver is to help them create the mindset they want before going on track.

Every driver likes to feel confident, focused and relaxed when they are going into qualifying or a race. So they will be more open to receiving ways for doing this than most other areas.

Pre-race routines have become very popular now. I remember doing it with drivers back in the day before it was an accepted thing to do, when drivers would sometimes feel shy to visualise laps, skip rope or do physical work in front of others. But now when you walk through the paddock there are bloody flexible bands pinging and tennis balls flying all over the place.

Drivers will have also have seen the Moto GP riders and F1 drivers doing their pre-race routines so all of a sudden it's a cool thing to do.

So I want you to capitalise on this open-mindedness with drivers now. This is your chance to help your driver create the emotions they want before they take to the track, and show them they can heavily influence their state of mind.

Resist telling them what to do driving-wise while warming them up – because they may see this as Mom or Dad telling them what to do again (depending on your relationship with them). Focus more on getting them in the right place mentally. Fill them with confidence and help them relax into what's coming up.

As you are warming up with them, you could even get them to talk you through their game plan: how they are going to drive or how they will approach this session or race. Doing this along with some form of exercise will really help them create the correct mindset and emotions.

To get the best out of themselves they must be focused yet relaxed, confident but not ego-driven. They just need to feel in the rhythm and think about certain process-related goals (not results) they want to meet out there. You or their coach can help them do this as they are warming up.

Once they can see this works, they may be even more open to controlling their emotions in other areas of their racing. They may want to change their emotions on track, they may want to create certain emotions in the debrief room and so on.

Changing emotions on the go

It's one thing getting mentally prepared before you go on track, but a lot happens in the time between drivers leaving the pitlane and taking the chequered flag.

They may go into a race feeling good, but this can change as they line up on the grid or when they have just lost yet another position during the race.

This means they must continuously manage their emotions while they drive, which is yet another skill to master.

Here are just a few on-track scenarios that can easily knock a driver off their emotional game:

1. Having to deliver a lap in qualifying
2. Being pressured by a driver who is close behind
3. Driving as fast as they can yet noticing they are still not producing competitive lap times
4. Struggling with a poor handling car during a long race or in a battle with other drivers
5. Refocusing after making a mistake
6. Being forced off by another driver
7. Seeing their championship rival pulling away from them
8. Worrying about what things look like from the outside and how other people will view it
9. Being in a race-winning position for the first time
10. Having a terrible first lap of a race

All these things and more can happen during a single race event and it's up to the driver to be able to remain emotionally in control and have the required mindset activated in order for them to deal with all these challenges.

Obviously they need the driving skill, but if they can use their mind effectively they can at least reach their best level. That's all we can ask once the racing has begun.

This means they often have to keep managing their emotional state out there.

Disrupt things

Even though we seem to operate on autopilot where our preloaded values and beliefs form our Mental Matrix (mental model), it doesn't mean we cannot disrupt this and create new ways of reacting to things and behaving in those moments.

Let's say your driver's Matrix is set up in a way that causes them to become overly nervous when a race is about to start. If you can see this is hampering their performance, this needs to be changed or the energy from those nerves needs to be converted into a more helpful emotion.

You can help them overcome their nerves in two ways. First you can have a conversation with your driver to understand where the nerves are coming from and what particular fear is causing them. This is done way before the event itself so the driver has time to understand why their mind is 'freezing' on them and they can confront the fears they have.

This is a process I am sure you have already gone through with your driver on different topics, so you will know how to do this. But essentially it is getting them to understand why they get nervous and giving them an alternative perspective that helps them deal with these nerves.

I did this conversationally to myself when I was racing because I was one of those drivers who got too nervous prior to a race. I couldn't even eat breakfast on race morning, hence why I started to learn mental sciences because I wanted to overcome these kinds of automatic reactions.

However, one day as I was waiting on the grid, probably shaking like a shitting dog, I said to myself:

"You know what Enzo? You are hating this feeling right now but there will come a day when you will miss these nerves. You are lucky to have something you care about so much that causes this feeling. Your Dad never feels this kind of adrenaline – and neither do most people. This is a privilege dude, make the most of it!"

This one conversation that I had with myself completely changed my life. From that point forward I was super-excited before races. Later in my racing life I was even too relaxed, to the point where I was late to the car because I was nonchalantly taking my time getting ready.

I found it hard to believe a simple thought could change me so much, but it did. I simply changed my perception because it made sense to me. I was obviously ready to change and this thought tipped me over the edge. I modified my belief system and more importantly, I updated my Matrix.

You can do something similar with your driver. It may have to come from them to really make the penny drop, but I hope my experience of changing things will encourage you to have some quality conversations with your driver, leading them towards similarly helpful conclusions.

The ABC Technique

The second way to help your driver control their emotions on track is a mental training strategy I enjoy teaching, called the ABC Technique.

It is common to see a driver in a race looking composed and in control as they tick off the laps, only for their race to take a sudden turn that thrusts them into a whirlwind situation where they mentally crumble. A driver can be completely fine one moment and in turmoil the next.

It's common to see this happen with players in other sports like tennis and even team sports like football. As a spectator you can physically see one player or one side performing confidently and in the zone, but if they make a few mistakes you witness their mental energy change. Then their opponent becomes the one who starts to mentally perform well. It's as if they are exchanging mindsets and in turn the momentum of the game swings between them.

A race driver has to deal with this emotional game of tennis in most of their races. A top performing driver is good at dealing with these moments and they can maintain a consistent mental state even as they are thrown certain challenges.

When I say challenges I mean things like dealing with pressure, regaining their focus after making a mistake, getting back into mode after being overtaken, etc. All these moments can easily create automatic responses from drivers and they can quickly spin out of control mentally.

This is a death rattle to any driver's career because professional race teams and manufacturers need drivers to be consistent and to perform week in week out in a dependable way. So if your driver is struggling in this area, it's time to take immediate action.

This is where I want to introduce you to the ABC Technique. It is designed to help drivers regain their mental focus and manage their emotions on the fly.

If you head to my YouTube channel called *The Race Driver Coach Show* or Google *'Episode 3 - How to change your emotions in car ABC technique'* you will find a video where I run through how to use this mental technique, but I will also explain it here.

The goal of the ABC Technique is to help drivers come up with a way for them to jump from one emotional state to another.

They do this by disrupting their current emotion or thought process – and assertively, if not aggressively, putting another emotion or thought process in its place.

This is another surface mental technique and a quick fix but I have found it very useful for myself and my clients.

The term ABC is obviously an acronym and stands for:

- A = Awareness
- B = Break
- C = Change

By using this technique, we are getting the driver to first become **aware** that they are in an emotion they do not want to be in. Once they come to terms with that, they need to dramatically **break** their pattern of thought and immediately **change** their emotional equation to create another emotion or mental state.

Let's say a driver notices their lap time is not good enough and the drivers behind them are starting to close in on them. Our driver then pushes more and makes a mistake. Due to that error, they look in the mirror and they see the other drivers even closer than before.

Our driver starts to panic, finding it hard to even drive correctly. They know the pace is in the car but they are operating and driving in a way that is causing the slower pace and mistakes.

Our driver can go one of two ways here. They can either continue as they are and eventually get overtaken. This will probably see them storm off into the truck after the race, throwing their helmet around and maybe even blaming the car for its lack of pace.

Or they can use the ABC Technique in an attempt to get their mind back in the game as they drive.

If they are to use the ABC Technique they would interject things.

They have still seen their uncompetitive lap times, they have made the mistake, they are starting to panic due to the other cars now getting even closer, but instead of allowing that panic to continue, they:

First: Realise they are panicking (aware) - This will all be done quickly but they still need to be aware that they are in a state of mind that is not helpful so they want to change it.

They can even say to themselves "I'm getting stressed right now, let's get back into it."

Second: They break their pattern - Being aware they are in a certain unwanted mental state can be enough on its own, but the driver now needs to do something that disrupts their thought process and causes the brain to think "What's going on?"

To do this the driver needs to be in a safe place on track, like a straight, and they need to do something verbally or physically that shakes them out of their current mental mode. I've had some drivers smack the front of their helmet with the palm of their hand to shake themselves out of it or even say things like "Children are starving in Africa".

That last one sounds politically incorrect but this was a driver who was suffering from anger issues. Just by saying that sentence to themselves, they not only confused the mind but they suggested to their mind that they should be grateful for being able to race in the first place. It was their quickest way of changing their perspective and disrupting their angry thoughts.

It sounds crazy but now you know what I mean when I say that your driver must do something that breaks them out of their current train of thought.

This is a lot easier to do for people who are not in control of a vehicle that's travelling at 200kph, so the driver must do something that shocks them out of their thought process but doesn't put them at risk on the track.

Saying something outlandish or doing a quick, easy action is enough for a driver while they drive.

When you break your train of thought, your mind will look to make sense of things and it will search for some kind of answer because it is temporarily confused by what has just happened. It is in this very space in time where the driver must quickly put in place the emotion they really want.

Third: Change their emotion - The driver will quickly change their perspective and how they use their body while the brain is open.

The driver must change what they are focusing on and align their physiology (as explained earlier in the chapter) with the emotion they want.

For example, if they are making mistakes and getting frustrated, once they are aware of that frustration they should say or do something outlandish that breaks their pattern. Then they can immediately put a smile on their face (this already takes the mind to a different place), relax their arms a little and say out loud "Next corner!"

This is breaking the frustrated mindset and changing their focus and body to create a different emotion.

As they approach the next corner, they should remind themselves what is important about that corner driving-wise... and execute.

What they are doing here is changing their physiology and telling the mind what to focus on. All of this together produces a different emotion.

This is just an example of what drivers can do, but your driver can invent their own way of creating emotions and using the ABC Technique.

it may all sound a lot but when your driver has this down, they will do the whole technique within two or three seconds.

Weightlifters do this

This ABC Technique is similar to the mental 'pump-up' procedure we see weightlifters use before they step onto the stage during a competition.

They have to go from their relaxed state of mind (created as they wait patiently backstage) to complete beast mode within seconds. You will often see their trainer screaming at them, slapping them around the face or hitting them hard on the back whilst the athlete themselves screams back and takes a big sniff of ammonia.

This is their BC of the ABC Technique: their trigger that it's show time as they mentally prepare to lift a personal best and fight for the win.

Actors, athletes, public speakers and pretty much anyone else who needs to perform on demand all do something that helps them achieve their optimal state of mind.

Many race drivers also do this prior to getting into the car, but they also may need to do it again on the go if they lose their way and want to reignite their focus.

That's why I added the 'A' for awareness, because the driver must first realise when it is time to pull their mental trigger; then pull it.

Practise this first

I strongly recommend that you get your driver to practise their ABC prior to using it in a race. A test day or a practice session would be a good time because they need to be comfortable with it and create something that works for them.

The more they do it, the better they will get at it – until it gets to the point where they only need to take a deep breath or do some other subtle movement in order to change their emotions while they compete. The more we do something, the deeper ingrained it becomes. And once they get better at this, they may even shorten the whole process and get even better at switching emotions.

Like every change we make mentally, it is a very conscious process to start with and it will feel awkward. But the more they commit to it, the better they get.

In essence, once they know they must change their current mindset, they shock the brain to break the current pattern. Then they quickly deploy the emotion they want by changing their focus and their physiology – and away they go...

Going deeper

It goes without saying that some of the emotions your driver may be struggling to manage may require a deeper level of work or training. Maybe they have had certain unpleasant experiences in life that continue to affect their mental state now, or they have certain fears that are difficult for them to overcome.

If so, the surface work I have explained so far in this chapter can still work in the short term but you may want to also consider hiring a good mental coach or sports psychologist to help them further.

It can be difficult to find a mental coach or psychologist who is not only good at what they do, but they can also gel with your driver and get the most out of your them. But they are out there.

Shop around, ask people in the industry if they can recommend someone who is good at what they do, and do your research.

Many drivers do not like the stigma of going to see a psychologist but if they are specific to sport or brand themselves as a mental trainer/coach, you can communicate this to your driver as part of them leaving no stone unturned.

Communicate to them the importance of the mind, and that you are just going to a mental coach to help them use more of their mind. I must admit people are more open to this now but if it requires a perspective change, you could be the person to do that for them.

I started training myself in the mental side by going to mental performance seminars and I studied various mental sciences early on in my driving days. This is because I was looking for the advantage in every area.

Your driver will hopefully get to – or be at – a stage where all the drivers are at a similar level in terms of driving skill. When you get near the top it is always like this. Then you notice the driving is no longer the differentiator, the mental aspect is.

Your driver must understand this and take advantage of it before it's too late.

The mind controls everything we do, so why wouldn't they want to program their internal computer better than their competitors?

CHAPTER 11
IMPROVE THEIR CONFIDENCE

Confidence is a subject that I have always been fascinated by. Even though it is a part of our mental game and heavily responsible for how our lives turn out, most of us are not taught how to manage it consciously.

I would go as far as saying that if you want to improve your life in some way, whether personal or professional, confidence is one of the most important areas to master.

I would also say self-confidence is one of the easiest things that you can change and manipulate.

This is great news – but due to it being something that can easily be manipulated, it also means our confidence levels can easily be knocked and they can fluctuate as we go through life. It's an ever-moving needle within our minds that can help or harm our progress and fulfilment in life.

If you are like me, you may well have experienced various levels of confidence as you went through different periods of your life.

For me, I was confident up to the age of about 10 years old. Up to that age I would constantly be acting the fool to make my parents laugh and dancing like Michael Jackson in public (he was my hero when I was younger...)

However, my level of confidence changed between the ages of 11 to 15 years old, when I was more worried about fitting in at high school rather than being my true self.

I would find it very difficult to read out loud in front of the class and I would dread anything that would potentially expose me to public judgement.

Then near the end of high school I changed once again. All of a sudden I came back out of my shell. I started to put myself out there more and I was mixing with the so-called 'popular' kids at school. I remember them asking myself: "Where have you been all these years?"

My yoyo transition in confidence during this period has always intrigued me and it was partially responsible for igniting my interest in human behaviour and mental performance.

This also motivated me to help others become more confident. I fully understood the pain we live through when we want to achieve something, but we feel trapped or paralysed just because of the mental hurdles we have (things like lack of confidence or fear of failure).

I view confidence (along with fear of failure) as being an area we must seriously get a hold on if we are to improve our lives, our careers and our results.

We all have our own meaning attached to confidence depending on the context, but for this chapter I want to refer to confidence as a word that describes someone who has genuine self-belief, who performs freely without hesitation, who can engage with others well and someone who welcomes constructive criticism.

In short, confidence is the ability to be yourself and to be free mentally.

When a driver has this kind of confidence, they trust their own ability to deal with whatever challenge presents itself and they care less about what others think about them.

If I were to describe someone who has all these traits and demonstrates the type of confidence I am referring to here, I can't think of a better example than... wait for it... Forrest Gump.

Even though Forrest is a fictional character, if I had a scale of confidence that gauged people from 1 to 10, I'd like to change that scale so it read: 1 to Gump.

When you are confident you trust yourself more and throw yourself into situations with less thought of the consequences. In doing so you let yourself go for things in life and when you do, you are more likely to perform with a more resourceful mind.

There is less "What if?" and more "Why not?"

When a driver has low confidence levels

It is easy to see when a driver is lacking confidence both on or off track.

When watching a driver who is not confident as they drive, you will notice them:

- Looking overly nervous if they have a high starting position for a race
- Looking behind them or in the mirrors too often during the race
- Hesitating when an overtaking opportunity presents itself
- Allowing the car or kart to bully them around the track instead of driving assertively

- Talking about how close the walls are to the edge of the track, which then causes them to lose time through those certain sections

Outside the car, you can notice when a driver isn't bursting with confidence when:

- Their body language looks more like a scared cat rather than a person with intention
- They don't speak up or they dread it when it's their turn to talk in front of others
- They shy away from talking to a team boss or a sponsor
- They avoid eye contact while talking to others
- They find it hard to make critical decisions

These are all obvious observations but some drivers who struggle with confidence actually react in other ways. You may hear them speaking loudly in the race truck, or boasting about their previous race results, lap times or overtaking manoeuvres. These drivers use bravado to disguise their lack of confidence and their ego tries to protect them in this way.

We recognise this as a driver who has some insecurities, but it's all linked to their confidence.

No matter how drivers react when they lack confidence, each and every observation that I have just mentioned can be detrimental to their performance and their career. It can especially hurt their ability to be a leading figure in their team or in the sport itself.

They are simply not acting in a way that helps them towards their goals.

A confident driver leads a team

When a driver walks into the team environment, people within that team should view them as being 'the boss'. There will be a team boss already, but the driver is the one who can really make magic happen. They should be the person who sets the standard for the overall atmosphere of the team.

If you read about any true champion in sport you will notice they had a strong character when competing. Each of them had their own flaws and personal hang-ups (because they are human) but when it's game time or they are training, they run the show.

Their confidence may dip from time to time but they take it upon themselves to steer the collective mindset and act as the heart of their team or squad.

Over the years I have had the pleasure of working with drivers who had this level of confidence and one such driver who comes to mind is Jack Hawksworth – who, by the way, is one of the quickest and most well-rounded drivers I've had the privilege to work with.

Jack came to a team where I was coaching during an official post-season test in Abu Dhabi. When he arrived at the team garage for the preparation day I noticed that within the first half hour, he had already managed to get the team around his little finger.

Even though we had two other drivers also doing their seat fitting at the same time, for some reason most of the team members were gathered around his car.

They were listening intently to him as he explained what he wanted adjusted on the seat and within the cockpit. He was direct with his instructions and he knew exactly what he wanted. He attracted attention just by the way he communicated and because of his overall demeanour.

This caught my attention because when he spoke, the team members really listened and when he wanted something, they enthusiastically got it for him. He had them eating out of his hand. When I see him now all these years later, I notice he still has that ability to get a team around him.

How important do you think this is?

This is why I preach what I preach... because I have seen many examples of drivers who have this confidence and they have all achieved successful careers.

Confidence, like work ethic, is yet another area that most drivers fall short on. So this is yet another area that I advise your driver to work on so they can increase their chances for success and stand out from other drivers.

Exceptions and alter egos

There are obviously exceptions to what I have just said – because we have all seen successful individuals in every sport and sector who aren't naturally confident people. But when it comes to them performing within their arena (like in a race car, on stage, on the court, in the boardroom, etc) they become a different person and they still manage to perform at their best.

You will know of drivers who seem to be very shy in the awning, yet once they put that helmet on they turn into an animal. These drivers feel at home on track and can fully express themselves; they feel free when driving.

Many of us are introverts. An introvert isn't necessarily someone who lacks confidence, they may just have a reserved character trait and they don't feel the need to be outspoken or social. They may like their own company and feel quite content by themselves. An introverted person can still have high levels of confidence, but they may not demonstrate it externally as they simply dislike taking part in small talk.

This is something to keep in mind when you are 'psychoanalysing' your own driver. They could well be the type of person who is private or naturally quiet and they just don't want to be the centre of attention. They are not scared to stand out but they just don't feel the need to.

Believe it or not, Michael Jordan, Keanu Reeves, Lady Gaga, Jeff Bezos, Jay-Z and even Elon Musk are self-confessed introverts.

We see them as these big characters who have all rocked their respective industries – but remember that when we see them, they are on their stage. Michael Jordan becomes a different beast when he is on the court or in the changing room, Lady Gaga becomes a flamboyant butterfly when she hits the stage and Elon Musk can be seen doing his dad dancing when launching a new product or walking the red carpet.

When it's Go-Time or show time for these people, they summon their alter ego to take over and they do what needs to be done.

With this in mind, we cannot ignore the natural personality of your driver. If you feel your driver is introverted then we cannot expect them to suddenly become a Conor McGregor or Muhammad Ali personality type in life.. Instead we need to help them create an alter ego that they can call upon when needed.

I like to teach drivers how to create and use their alter ego because some drivers are ultra-confident in the race truck but they lose that confidence as soon as they sit in the race seat. So they need to learn how to feel self-assured when competing.

Meanwhile other drivers act like demons while they're on track but when they're out of the car they act more like mice. This causes them to be overshadowed by teammates and it doesn't help them inspire their team or their sponsors.

Either way, it is very common for drivers to have the need to consciously shift their mindset when it comes to competition time.

We are not just talking about when the driver is on track here; there are many different situations that drivers are exposed to when they are required to quickly create a different state of mind. For instance, they may need to react accordingly when a microphone or camera gets shoved in their face at short notice, and from time to time they will have to stand up for themselves and voice their opinions within the team.

We must never ignore a driver's natural character because they need to be themselves, but they may sometimes need to adjust to the situation they are in and act in a way that helps them get what they want. This all requires a certain level of confidence and the ability to kick into a different personality when needed.

Confidence is just an emotion

When I quiz confident people about how they operate in such a way, most of them tell me it was something they developed over the years. They weren't always that way but over time they figured out how to believe in themselves more. Due to their life experiences they built this mental state that we label as confident.

For some, it was the demands forced upon them by life itself: they lived through challenging times when they simply had to step up if they were to survive it. They were in a 'sink or swim' situation and by choosing to swim they learned this was the best way to be and things progressed from there. Before they knew it, confidence was a given and a necessity for them.

Other people who operate with confidence told me it was something they had to consciously learn to do. They understood how and who they needed to be in order to get more from themselves, so they took it upon themselves to develop their required state of mind.

Some people have told me they were born with confidence and they have always had an outlook that helps them let loose and be themselves.

No matter how all of these people created confidence or became more confident, each time I quiz them I make sure I delve deeper... to understand their beliefs and what strategies they use to get themselves there.

When doing this I always seem to come to the same conclusion, that confidence is nothing more than a simple emotion.

This is great news because (as I talk about in the emotions chapter) we can control or at least heavily influence our emotions and our mindset. We are the ones who get to design our Mental Matrix and we can learn how to change our emotions.

I recommend that you do not skip the emotions chapter because when it comes to improving your driver's confidence, the Perspective and Body formula (how emotions can be seen as a mathematical equation) and even the ABC Technique can be of great use to them.

Having said that, for the rest of this chapter I will share the techniques and processes I use with my drivers to further help them improve their confidence.

The steps for improving confidence

It is always a very individual journey when helping someone improve their mental skills and emotional control. But as this book needs to help everyone, I obviously cannot make this section bespoke to your son or daughter. So instead I will give you a templated step-by-step structure that you can adjust and fit to your needs.

The good thing about mental training is that you can use whatever suits you as an individual and mould things accordingly.

We now have many therapies and mental sciences out there, and what works for one person may not work for the next. So whether it is my coaching blueprint or anyone else's, always be open-minded and take the parts that fit for you – and even get creative by developing your own way to improve yourself (or your child) mentally.

Here is the general outline for how I approach helping drivers improve their confidence.

Step 1 – Expose the need to change

Just as with work ethic, before we can expect anyone to change their mental processing or behaviour we need to make sure they are coming into this with motivation.

As with everything in life, if we want to make a big change mindset comes first. Whether someone wants to improve a personality trait, quit smoking or be more proactive, they need to have a sense of urgency and determination to make it happen.

They need to convince you that they must change and improve their confidence. This happens when they open their eyes to the fact that their lack of confidence is killing their career or making it impossible for them to move forward.

The best sign for when a driver is truly motivated to change something is when they say things like: "I need to change things, I must change and I must do it now!"

Where they verbally communicate this to you or whether you can tell they are thinking that through their body language, they need to reach that level.

I do this by getting them to walk me through the current challenges they are facing. This could be their fear of approaching a prospective sponsor, talking to a team boss, attacking high speed corners or making overtaking moves on track.

If the challenge that they are not comfortable with is hampering their progress, as you discuss this with them you can ask "How would you prefer for things to have played out?" or "What do you wish you'd done differently?"

What you are doing here is getting them to tell you the real problem. The actual challenge itself is nearly irrelevant because it will come in different guises, so it's the core personal challenge that we are looking to identify here. You want to find out what is really holding them back.

They may start with an external challenge like "I wish I had been more aggressive in the race" or "I should have spoken to that team boss when I had the chance." If so this is your time to identify the real issue and help them understand they can take those actions and be who they want to be; but first they need to build the kind of person who can take these actions naturally.

The actual conversation I have with a driver will go something like this:

Driver – "I can't believe I didn't talk to that team boss"

Enzo – "What stopped you?"

Driver – "I didn't know what to say."

Enzo – "Well, what do you actually want to know from them?"

Driver – "I want to know if I could drive for their team next year!"

Enzo – "Ok, well why didn't you ask them that?"

Driver – "I didn't want to bother them."

Enzo – "You certainly achieved that... but I bet you regret not speaking up now, don't you?"

Driver – "Yes."

Enzo – "That was probably your last chance of seeing them before next year, so basically you blew your one chance to get their attention. If you could do it all again now and have a second chance, would you talk to them?"

Driver – "Hell yeah!"

We would then continue this conversation and I would ask the driver what the real reason for them not talking to the team boss was. And they would eventually admit something like "I didn't want to come across the wrong way and make a fool of myself."

Then, after digging further, we would eventually come to the conclusion that the driver lacks confidence – and some of that stems from how they worry about what others think about them.

Having an honest and non-judgemental conversation like this can take you down many different roads but all too often it leads to one of the most important things in the driver's life: the truth.

Also, just as importantly, it helps the driver generate motivation to change or improve something about themselves.

Like I already alluded to, the fuel for change must come from the person themselves. They have to see how much their behaviour is holding them back from what they most want.

Going back to this example conversation, if I wanted the driver to change their ways, I would get them to explain to me what their racing career will look like next year if they were to continue to not approach team bosses.

I would carry that timeline on (to add more pain to the situation) and ask what their career will look like in three years if they continue to let their lack of confidence stand in their way.

This is all with the aim of getting the driver to the point where they fully understand that they MUST change. That's called motivation.

If you are having a conversation with your driver like this, then adding a small sprinkling of regret is another layer that creates motivation. If they were to explain or be reminded of all the past times they allowed their confidence to prevent them from taking action, they can paint a mental picture of where they would be now if they hadn't allowed that to happen.

You obviously need rapport with your driver to have this kind of conversation because it can easily be interpreted as you being judgemental. So make sure you build rapport with them and deliver your questions with love.

Once a person gets the motivation by adding enough pain to the way they have been behaving – and on top of that you show them how good life can be if they do change things – then they will usually do something about it.

This is exactly what the three ghosts did for Scrooge in the story *A Christmas Carol.* They showed him his past to understand why he is the way he is now, they showed him his present life to see how things are going from a different perspective, and they showed him how things are going to play out if he continues on that path.

This for me is the most powerful way to help someone understand what needs to change in their life and to help them get to a place – mentally – where they are ready to take action.

When a driver realises their minor fears are causing them to behave in a way that causes them to live their major fear (failing to reach their racing goals) they will decide it's time to change.

As a parent or coach, you first need to get them to that place.

Step 2 – Come up with challenges

Once they believe that gaining more confidence is an absolute must, you can offer your assistance and agree that you are going to help them grow their comfort zone over the coming months.

Both of you will come up with small tasks that will cause them to step outside their comfort zone and force them to work out their confidence muscles.

If applicable, the very first task could be asking them to prepare an email that will actually be sent to a team boss, where they are the one who (once you have spell checked it) actually presses 'send'.

This is putting them into the driver's seat in more ways than one, helping them see their actions can carry some weight, and they are the person who took control and created that action. They did it.

This is an obvious observation to most people. But for those who struggle with confidence, realising that they can be heard and their actions can cause a reaction in the big wide world can help them feel more in control and more powerful as an individual.

This is what can be known as a Confidence Building Block.

The next day you could both set up a challenge where your child has to sort out all the food when you go to a restaurant or a takeaway. They are the ones who have to make the order and pay for it.

Ordering food within a crowded pizza parlour is quite a challenging task for someone who is shy, but it's a great place to start. If your driver has already passed this stage you could both choose an even more challenging task, like getting them to strike up a conversation with a prospective sponsor.

These constant challenges are a great way to teach them they can do whatever they want in life, and along the way they will actually be picking up life skills that will help them.

It will show your driver things are never as scary as they may seem. That's the epiphany we want them to have by doing these challenges.

When doing this you will learn more about your driver and you can help them with advice about how they can best phrase things or hold themselves. As long as they believe you are working with them and not judging them, this will work well.

You can give them constructive feedback, demonstrate how to possibly do it next time and use it to experiment things together. You could even show them how you do it beforehand to give them an idea of how to talk to people or tackle the current day's challenge.

When I do this with a driver I usually work with them to come up with monthly or weekly challenges that they must complete in between our coaching sessions. When they do achieve these challenges we talk them through and see what can be learned and adapted.

Parents are in the perfect position to do exactly the same with their children. As long as your child is determined to improve – and they trust that you are aligned with them and not judging them – they will be open enough to give this a go. If you think they will fight this approach then, like I said earlier, do this more subtly so you coach them on the go without them even realising.

Step 3 – Help them learn how to produce confidence on demand

Again, please read through the emotions chapter to see how your driver can change and create the emotion known as confidence on the go.

Help them change their perspective about a certain situation and show them how to hold their body in a confident manner.

Challenge them to create different emotions on demand to sharpen their skills and help them realise they actually have the power to produce the mindset (emotions) they want, when they want it.

This can be done prior to each challenge you set them. Using the team boss example, if you get them to focus on what they want from that boss and how fun it will be to talk to them – and on top of that you get them to approach the boss with their shoulders slightly back, head up with a big beaming smile on their face – you are teaching your driver how to create confidence there and then.

If they fail to do this by letting their mind go back to their old negative thought patterns, or they drop their shoulders and have that petrified look on their face, you can show them how that 'Perspective and Body' caused the emotion known as fear.

That's perfect. It just goes to show they can create emotions on demand. Now they just have to do it with confidence instead of fear.

Creating emotions is fun. It is something we can all do. If you teach your driver (your child) how to do this, it can be life-changing for them.

Practical confidence exercises

On top of creating the motivation to change, challenges and teaching them how to create emotions, I want to share with you some other mental exercises you can do with your driver that may help.

Exercise 1 - Mental rehearsal

If it helps, you can also role play or get your child to mentally rehearse certain situations they currently struggle with.

If they find it hard to talk confidently in interviews or even talk to people one-to-one, you could get them to run through things in their mind beforehand.

If they are soon to be speaking on camera, ask your driver to close their eyes and imagine they are talking to the interviewer with a smile on their face, feeling excited to share their story. They can see themselves looking confident, chatting away and enjoying it.

If we show the mind the kind of future we want, especially when it comes to how we want to act, our mind is much more likely to do just that. It at least helps us to paint the situation differently in our mind's eye, which is important because we often create pictures in our minds that scare us. So we may as well practise doing it the other way, right?

Public speakers do this prior to an event. They will use mental rehearsal to see the crowd as having smiles on their faces and they will see themselves as enjoying the talk. They then turn up ready to share their story or have a conversation with the audience, instead of feeling as though they are there to perform.

When people fear public speaking (yes, I have spoken to plenty of them too) they often visualise the audience with judgemental eyes and imagine them as being bigger than they really are. This causes the speaker to feel under pressure and worried about getting things wrong.

A lot of that fear was caused by how they were seeing the event in their mind's eye.

Mental rehearsal and visualisation may take some practice, because often people become frustrated when they cannot see things while visualising. If your driver struggles with this and it puts them off doing it, simply ask them to close their eyes and imagine the situation.

They don't need to actually see it, just pretend and imagine what it would look like.

Changing the word 'visualise' to 'imagine' can work wonders when helping someone mentally rehearse something that's coming up.

Like with emotions, have fun with this and help them paint the future in their mind as they want to see it. As long as it helps them feel more relaxed about things, it will work.

Even if they imagine the interviewer having big Mickey Mouse ears.

Exercise 2 - Create a trigger

An emotional trigger, often referred to as a Power Move, can be useful for a driver before they have to take action.

Using stage performers as an example again, they will be seen pulling some kind of emotional trigger backstage before going out to entertain the audience.

Some will pray, some will chant, others will execute physical movements. They do something that gets them into their peak mental state and jumpstarts the mindset they want to create.

This can be a great technique for drivers who want to create confidence quickly. Going back to the professional weightlifters, just moments before they attempt to bench their personal best in competitions they will pull their emotional trigger by performing their routine. It may be their trainer hitting them on the back whilst they scream at one another or the sniffing salts. Either way it shocks the brain into the mode the weightlifter wants and their mind knows exactly what to do next.

You don't need to do this with your driver, but it is good to have a trigger of their own that tells their mind it's Game Time.

This can be as subtle as them listening to music or as outlandish as what a weightlifter does. Both methods can be used for your driver to get into a confidence state.

This is not a false pump-up, but a practised routine that has been used over and over again and never fails to create the mindset your driver wants.

Due to our emotions being so led by what we think about and how we hold our body, I suggest that you create an emotional trigger with your driver that uses both mental and physical aspects.

For example, they can talk to themselves in a positive way, reminding themselves of how lucky they are to have this chance; then they can look forward to what is coming with a smile on their face. Or they can be more active by clapping their hands together or clenching their fist at the same time as shouting "Let's Go!"

Whatever they come up with, they have to use it over and over again to strengthen the bond between their actions and the state of mind they want to create.

I do this whenever I need to get into mode in order to perform. If I am driving to see a client I will sit bolt upright in the driver's seat listening to loud motivational videos on YouTube for the entire journey – even if the client is three hours' drive away... I will envisage how I want this session or meeting to play out and I will be focused on giving that client everything I have to help them.

Just before arriving I will pull my trigger – which is normally a thud on my chest with a clenched fist as I will firmly say the word "Yes" with a smile on my face.

My mind will know exactly what that means and I will burst through those doors ready to change someone's life.

This all sounds aggressive and over the top, but it is honestly how I create the mindset I want. Depending on what challenge I am helping a driver with, I will adjust the tone and be congruent with them, but this is my long-form emotional trigger.

Once you have some kind of trigger or routine in place and you use it over and over again, it becomes reinforced and automatically aligns your mind with the activity you are just about to partake in.

You will see Valentino Rossi's ritual before getting on the bike and Rafael Nadal's ritual prior to each serve. This process uses their mental muscle memory to create their flow state.

This can also be used for your driver when they have to access confidence and the 'Just Do It' mentality.

So create a trigger, pull the trigger and go.

Experiment

If you couple what was spoken about in this chapter with what we covered in the emotions chapter, you will have a few weapons at your disposal that can help your driver improve their confidence.

Due to each of us learning and translating things in our own ways, you can experiment with mental exercises that may help your driver. I am sure that while you were reading this you will have already thought of what to try and different ways in which you can introduce things.

Don't hold back. You know your driver better than anybody so feel free to adapt what I have been writing about in this book. As long as your driver is keen to try things and they are not put in harm's way mentally or physically, come up with your own exercises.

At the end of the day we know why some people are confident. It largely comes down to how they view things, and their perspective on certain actions that need to be taken. They will focus on the activity first (what needs to be done) and they will often overlook how they actually feel about doing it. Their feelings take a back seat and are often irrelevant to them.

By contrast a person who lacks confidence often does the exact opposite. They prioritise the feelings they have about a certain action way before they entertain actually doing it. This creates apprehension and self-doubt.

A driver who struggles with their confidence levels may just have a fear of failure, not being enough or being judged. The judgement side of things is especially prominent in younger drivers because they can still possess the school playground mindset, where it is valuable to be the 'cool kid'. This can easily create a lack of confidence.

Like we said earlier, if they are fearful of failure or judgement this can often be worked on via conversations between the two of you to help them change their perspective and to feel loved no matter what results they get.

When I say results I don't just mean racing results obviously, I mean in anything they do on any given day. They really need to understand that failing is learning, so in some ways they need to fail more in order to progress. Life is a numbers game.

Fill their Confidence Bucket

I want you to pretend that we all have our very own bucket of confidence stoCed within us, and it is our duty to keep that bucket topped up.

If it is full, then we feel supremely confident.

If it is empty, we lack the confidence even to leave the house each day.

To keep filling this bucket up, we must genuinely focus the mind on thoughts that help us create confidence. However, our Confidence Bucket also has holes in the bottom of it... so this confidence is constantly leaking out.

Each hole represents an opposing thought, belief or viewpoint which robs us of our confidence.

For example, somebody who suffers with severe lack of confidence will have huge holes in their bucket caused by them believing the following:

- I am not good enough
- I do not deserve to be in the position I am in
- I really fear failing so I want to avoid it
- I don't want to look stupid in front of others
- I care what other people think of me

These kinds of beliefs and viewpoints burn big holes in the bottom of a person's Confidence Bucket. So no matter how much they try and pump themselves up or how often people tell them they are worthy and loved, the leaks are too big for their Confidence Bucket to remain full.

Confidence is leaving their bucket quicker than it's being put in.

This is the same for any positive emotion we have, like love, gratitude, happiness, serenity, etc. I like to think these all have their own bucket that we must keep full if we are to experience them.

If your driver is constantly focusing on their fear of failure, telling themselves they are not worthy or worrying about being judged, each of these will cause a hole in their Confidence Bucket and none of the positive statements you tell them will have much impact. Their holes are simply too big.

If this is the case for your driver, you need to help them address the things that rob them of their confidence, and provide them with more confidence – via mental training or teaching them how to deal with things.

As parents or coaches it is up to us to help fill the internal Confidence Bucket that our drivers have within them. They will always have some holes in the bottom because you can never fully cut out their past experiences or negative thoughts, but we need to help them make those holes smaller by controlling those negative viewpoints.

We must also feed them with more confidence to keep things topped up.

This isn't about overinflating their ego with compliments to give them a deluded reality; it is showing them through experiences (via the challenges you set them and the lessons they take on) that they are fully capable of taking action and giving them the small wins to teach their mind they are indeed a powerful human being.

Your driver, you and me will always have times when our confidence is knocked. Life does that; it causes us to question ourselves, which then slowly eats at us and at the bottom of our Confidence Bucket. But it's important for us to keep patching up those leaks and resetting our outlook on life so it serves us.

So the next time you hear your driver use language that beats their confidence down, I want you to imagine those very words have just created another hole in the bottom of their Confidence Bucket. It's up to you to catch them when they do this, asking them what they mean by those self-defeating words in order to shift their negative mindset into a positive one.

For example, if they try and complain about the amount of bad luck they always seem to have, you remind them of all the good luck they have also had. Take them down the route of being grateful for these challenges – and of even having the chance to race in the first place.

Be the person who always helps them bat away negative comments because, believe me, if they are verbalising negative thoughts, they are running that kind of thought through their mind over and over again.

You can learn a lot about people by the words and language they use. They give you an insight into how they are operating on the inside, so keep correcting them and helping them create a mindset that will automatically generate confidence.

It will take a while and they will object to you correcting them, but over time you will make an impact – and as they get older they will start to listen.

This means you must also watch your own language patterns around them. It is unrealistic to think you can help your driver be more confident if you are not confident yourself – or if you are not demonstrating confident behaviour.

So you may have to top up your own bucket first before helping them top up theirs. I know I have to do that when coaching somebody in this area.

Summary

I have bombarded you with various ways to help your driver improve their confidence levels, so scan through the chapter again if needed to pick out what you think would be applicable to your situation and your driver.

Due to confidence being such a big topic and the training for it being so individual, you may have further questions. So never hesitate to get in touch with me for more info or for some advice.

All the mental techniques detailed here are very 'surface level' training. If you need somebody to go deeper into the mind of your driver, remember you are never alone. There are plenty of sports psychologists and specialists near you who can offer some assistance.

I really hope there is something within this and the previous chapters that will help you shine a light on things when it comes to helping your driver perform at their best.

You are a super-parent for reading this and for taking such an interest in your child's well-being. If you work with them and help them learn these emotional skills, you will be giving them a gift for life.

They may not show their appreciation much at the moment, but one day they will realise your commitment and they will be eternally thankful.

CHAPTER 12
HANDLING BAD RESULTS

I've named this chapter using a term I don't actually believe in; that term is obviously 'Bad Results'.

You will hear people say "good result", "bad result", "ok result", "unexpected result", "poor result" and so on. They constantly put adjectives in front of the word 'result' in order to communicate their experience and to give an account of what happened.

I do this myself to help communicate with people, but really I don't actually believe there is any such thing as a bad result.

It may sound like I'm taking linguistics a little too seriously here... but if we are to truly help your driver improve their reaction to their results, we must start by helping them view things in the best way possible.

You will have heard this explanation before, but it's a coach's (and a parent's) job to help their driver understand there are no such things as good or bad results, there are only 'outcomes'.

Each result a driver produces in any given session or race is nothing more than the outcome that was created by an accumulation of many factors.

The way they perform, the decisions they make, their current skill level, the actions and skill levels of their competitors, the actions of their engineer, the competitiveness of their car and the situations that arise in a race all come together to create a certain outcome.

So if your driver is flying off the handle and attaching way too much emotion to their results, we need to help them see things for how they really are.

Perspective

Perspective is something you hear me talk about a lot. I do this because I believe perspective is yet another superpower we have. We have the ability to label things in ways that either serve us or that bring us down.

We get to create our own reality by how we internally translate things in life.

If a driver underachieves in a race and finishes dead last, they can decide this is the worst thing that could ever happen to them and the end of their career. Or they can welcome the result and use the information from that race to completely revolutionise their approach next time out.

When a driver has a perspective that allows them to learn from every outing, no matter what the result, they often become the type of driver who goes far in this sport. Seeing things this way gives them a more resourceful mind, which in turn helps them solve problems better and advance quicker.

It is important that we help your driver view their results in a more helpful way, because if they are to progress they must understand that the outcomes they produce are nothing more than feedback.

A driver should be fascinated with the results they get, and they should view their racing in the same way an inventor views their experiments.

An inventor will experiment over and over again until they get the outcome they want. If they don't, they will find out a certain truth and move on to the next project. No matter how passionate they are about their vision, they will see the results they get and understand why they got each one. They use that information to build or change things.

In my opinion a race driver needs to be the same. They too should understand how they produced a certain outcome, learn from each outing as if each time was an experiment, then adjust accordingly.

Can you imagine if top inventors were like most race drivers? If so they would be throwing tantrums, losing heart, losing confidence and taking each failed experiment personally.

It's safe to say we wouldn't even have the light bulb if Thomas Edison reacted this way to the 10,000 failed attempts he went through. He would have given up after about 50.

So if your driver is reacting badly to the results they are getting, it's time to change their perspective and how they approach their craft.

We need to help them to detach emotion from their results and see them instead as feedback.

Emotions

We are used to attaching a lot of emotions to results. As sports fans we scream at the TV when our team is losing and we cheer when they win. It's all very straightforward if you are a spectator: the competitor/team/driver/player either wins, loses or draws. As we watch this unfold, we label that particular event as a good or bad result. We then have an emotional reaction to this.

This kind of emotional attachment to results that either we or our sports teams get is ingrained within us from a young age. We see how our family and friends react to these sporting events and we follow suit. We sometimes go one step further and allow our ego and identity to get wrapped up in the results we (or they) get.

This is all OK when watching sport as a fan, because on some level we love the buzz sport provides and we enjoy the story of a game. The emotional journey sport takes us on is fun because we like to be on the edge of our seats cheering on our team – with the real risk that we might lose a particular match, especially when we are sharing the experience with thousands of other fans.

However, when we also attach too much emotion to our own results and we link our identity and ego to them too, we run the risk of seriously hampering our performance.

This is a very common way for drivers to be, because a lot of the time they wrap their self-worth in with their results. Some drivers even believe their results determine how much their parents actually love them.

You see this in the karting world a lot. Parents pour love into their child if they win or finish high up, then they mentally punish them and take that love and affection away if their child finishes a race lower than whatever they expected.

Even if this isn't actually true, the young driver still sees it that way.

Tough love can work well when helping a driver improve, but conditional love – where the driver feels like they are not enough – doesn't often work in the long run.

Parents play a big role in helping their children see their results in the best way because the parents are the people who the drivers want to impress the most in their world. As mentioned earlier, they might not act in a way that shows they care what you think, but every child wants to make their parents proud.

With this in mind, as the parent it is also important that you control your emotions when the driver has had an unrewarding result. You also should view each result as feedback and get straight to work no matter how things play out.

Due to us watching from the outside (parents and coaches) it is easy for us to react as we do when watching our sports team on TV. But we must remember this is different.

This is an area where coaches and parents must walk the talk and practise what they preach. It is easy for us to get carried away with the emotions and ego that results can influence, but we must resist this as much as possible.

It's great to jump around when they win; of course we all do that. But when the dial swings the other way we must not get too down in front of them.

Ego

From time to time we all let our ego take the mental driving seat, but if a driver is doing this a little too often I promise you it will become their downfall.

Ego takes many forms – and we can see a driver operating with too much influence from their ego when they...

- Over-celebrate their wins
- Link their self-worth to their results (or their social media likes)
- Become overly jealous of other drivers
- Overreact to other driver's actions on or off track
- Want to be the most liked person in the team
- Find it hard to take criticism
- Worry about their image a little too much
- Worry a lot about what others think about them
- Aren't great when under pressure

- Blame others or make excuses after they have underperformed

The list is long when it comes to how someone's ego manifests into the outside world – because it takes on many guises and it is linked to our fear of not being enough (or loved enough) in life. Our ego can protect us but when it comes to a driver who is attempting to forge a career, ego is usually detrimental to their progress.

For example, when a driver over-celebrates their wins or even rubs their victories in the face of others, you can guarantee the same driver is a very poor loser and easily influenced by their results.

You can also bet your bottom dollar that, due to them allowing their ego to act up in such a way, they easily lose their confidence when they are experiencing a prolonged period of not achieving the results they want.

It is vital that you and your driver do not fall for the same trap – because if this kind of reaction is happening after each race weekend your driver can only go so far in this sport.

There are many performance ceilings in place for a driver and ego is one low-level ceiling that must be removed if they are to create a successful career, or they want to get the best out of themselves.

All of this is as relevant to the driver as it is their parents.

Calibrate their expectations

One of the most common reasons why drivers become upset about their results is because they go into a race event with expectations that are not aligned with reality.

Virtually all the drivers on any given grid will want to win. They want to get pole position and be hailed as the best driver out there, but due to the fact there is only top step of the podium, nearly all of them come back home disappointed – and sometimes tearful.

It's one thing being disappointed due to them underperforming on their potential or because they made mistakes; that's normal. But it's a whole different thing when a driver comes back upset due to their lap time or finishing position not being what they expected or hoped for.

That's why I am a big advocate of focusing a driver's expectations on personal performance based goals, instead of results based goals.

I do this because I want to put the driver more in control of things. Aiming for a race win is nice, but for me the win will come if the driver performs well enough overall. That's why I want to keep them focused on their performance and have goals in that area, and let the results look after themselves. The result should be a result of how you performed, not something you just aim for.

If a driver performs well, if they help set up their kart or car well, if their race craft is on point, if they make good starts, if they make effective decisions in the seat, if they lead their team well, then they have a shot at bringing home the trophy.

They only have a shot, though. Because as you know, they can do everything correctly from their side but they could have another driver take them out of the race, or they could have a mechanical failure, or they could receive an unjust penalty that can steal the win away from them.

A result is partially out of your driver's control, so why would you have a high position as your expectation going into an event?

I recommend that you do the following with your driver. If you ask them what they want to achieve this coming race weekend and they reply with "a top five position" get them to reverse engineer what that would take. They should make a short list of performance-related goals that will make that top five position possible and keep them focused on those instead.

The weekend will then be judged a success or a failure based on whether they achieved their performance-related goals. The trophy or the top five position will be just a bonus.

Just so we are clear, performance-related goals are things like:

- Achieve my optimal mindset for qualifying
- Achieve my optimal mindset in the races
- Motivate my mechanic and engineer more
- Have a better tyre-warming procedure
- Be more assertive on the opening laps

Performance goals are the things that contribute to building a high-performing race event. That should be the true goal and expectation that your driver and the people around them have.

Post event

You know when you have fully got your driver to think this way – and when they are obsessed with mastering their craft – when you ask something like "How did the weekend go?" and they answer with something like "Really good... I managed to drive consistently, I improved my race craft and I learned more about how to set the car up."

Or they reply with "Not great... I am still making mistakes and I still haven't got my braking down for slow corners."

These are answers from a driver who is focused on their performance rather than the lap time or race results. It is music to my ears when a driver replies like this. Obviously I don't want them finishing last as they keep telling me they are improving after each round, but you hopefully get where I am coming from here.

It's much better to hear them reply this way compared to hearing a driver say something like "pretty good, I was only 0.3s off the P1."

That is a driver who is results based. We don't want this kind of answer.

So always ask your driver how a particular session or day went... and listen to how they word their answer. Then you can mind-read what their focus is on and help them correct this if needed.

Coach John Wooden's approach

Before we leave this chapter I want to share how one of the greatest basketball coaches of all time, John Wooden, used to train his players to be when it came to their results.

Coach Wooden would insist that his players should have the exact same behaviour and response coming off the court after the game, whether they won or lost.

He didn't want the spectators to be able to see whether they had won or lost by looking at the players. If they won, they had the same body language as when they lost.

This would help the players stay humble, it would help them remain resourceful when facing defeat, it would remove emotion so they would be less nervous at critical times, they wouldn't tense up as much and they wouldn't become defence-minded when leading.

There's a lot to be said for this.

Going up against a team like this, one that didn't react to you and didn't lose their minds when being beaten, would be like competing against a team of terminators. No matter what you threw at them and how much you were up in that game, they would just keep coming for you.

This is a great skill to help your driver learn. Teach them how to remain positive and focused, no matter how hard things are. They should stay focused on executing and being at their absolute best no matter what.

I don't think we can completely copy this in motorsport because people want to see you ecstatically happy when you win. But maybe it just means that your driver can still have a spring in their step and demonstrate a positive mindset even after they finish in fifteenth place, so others cannot tell if their race went well or not.

You watch how this helps them control their emotions more and aids them to be more consistent. It also affects the other drivers on the grid or within their own team if they see your driver react like this. It makes your driver seem impenetrable.

Your driver will seem unbreakable.

CHAPTER 13
FRIENDS, GIRLFRIENDS AND BOYFRIENDS

To close out the performance section of the book, let's turn our attention to something more personal.

As mentioned earlier, there comes a time when your cherished child goes from being that cute little human who looked up to you as being their superhero, to becoming an independent person who now leads their own life and barely even speaks to you anymore.

On top of this there also comes a time when your child or children start to prioritise the relationships they have with their friends, and in turn they begin to develop intimate relationships.

This is something that can cause a lot of worry for you as a parent because you have to trust your child's decisions for who they choose to spend their time with. This can be a hindrance because we all know just how influential friends, girlfriends or boyfriends can be.

Let's be honest here: this can also be an uncomfortable period for parents because it's a time when you realise you are becoming less significant in your child's life.

Things are fairly simple when your child was younger and they were heavily influenced by you –because you could keep them safe and help them remain on track. However, as they grow and reach their teenage years, they start to have their own objectives and they become determined to be their own person. Choosing what they do with their time and who they share it with is all part of this.

As you will have already found out, this is not exactly an easy transition to deal with. But how smoothly this all goes down depends on the relationship you have with your child and how they personally handle becoming an adult. It also depends on the company they choose to keep.

From a coach's perspective

As you can tell by the content I create, I push the importance of a strong work ethic. I put this area on a pedestal because I see it as the one area that differentiates champions from most other drivers.

So I take the personal relationships my drivers have pretty seriously, because nothing frustrates me more than when I see drivers squander or ignore their opportunity – just because they allow their relationships to distract them.

I know it's part of growing up and maybe something that most of us have done in the past – we have all had times when we have taken our eyes off the ball due to our relationships – but still this is an area that gets my back up and one that I have little patience for.

My story

In some ways it's funny that I get so frustrated when drivers become distracted by their personal lives because I did exactly that when I was younger.

Maybe it's because, deep down, I still regret my actions and I don't want others to do the same, so I become sensitive to it when I notice others doing it. Whatever the reason, I am now going to run you through my personal experience so we can align things and see if you can take something from it.

Wait a moment; let's go back a little further just to add context and give you a more complete snapshot of my life.

I was born in the Midlands, England in the Seventies. I lived my first few years on a council estate (UK version of 'the projects') with my parents Mario and Barbara and my older brother Don.

As the name suggests, my father is an immigrant from Italy who, back then, worked in a factory while my mother also worked jobs and raised us at home.

My father had the typical immigrant mindset, where he would spend every waking hour working to keep a roof over our heads and keep his personal dreams alive. As he was working double shifts in the factory he would daydream about opening his own pizza shop – because even though there were obviously pizza parlours everywhere in Italy, they were not too popular in the UK at that time.

He and my mother eventually decided to go for it and they opened up a pizza takeaway, which was typically named Mario's. Unexpectedly, this shop became an instant success where we saw people queuing down the street on opening night.

The shop continued to thrive and it wasn't long before we moved into a nice area and lived in a brand new four-bedroom house. My brother and I went from being in a state school to being enrolled into a private school. This was a big shift for us – and to say we didn't really fit in at the private school is an understatement – but we eventually adjusted.

In the space of a few years we went from a family who was just about scraping by financially to living what could be called the British Dream. We had a nice house, my parents had a car each and we kids were receiving a good education.

It was quite a privilege for me to watch my parents build this new life for us. My brother and I would spend many nights in the flat above the shop watching our black-and-white TV and listening to all the hustle and bustle downstairs.

Little did we know then, but my parents were demonstrating two very important aspects to us. First the importance of work ethic and second the fact that a person can achieve almost anything they want. Ironically these are the two main topics I spend my life reminding others about. Isn't it funny how things turn out?

Before long we had a new arrival to the family. My sister Serina was born and once again this gave us the opportunity to witness how my parents could deal with this extra responsibility while running the company. Looking back, it was pretty impressive.

However, this story took a turn.

The business did very well for quite a few years... right up until the day we opened up a restaurant in a particular town that wasn't ready for this type of food.

My parents bet everything on this shiny new restaurant. They sold their current pizza shop and put every penny we had into it. But year after year the tables remained empty and financially we were in the red.

This was absolutely heart-breaking for my father – and it ultimately caused my parents to make the difficult decision to file for bankruptcy.

Dreams are wonderful things for us humans. They enable us to strive for something that forces us to live outside our comfort zones and they help us grow as individuals. But boy, do they slap you in the face when things don't go to plan...

This was a very rough period for the Mucci family.

My parents managed to get back on their feet. They opened another pizza shop close to the original one, which did pretty well, but the turmoil of the business took its toll on my parents' relationship... and when I was around fifteen years old they divorced.

Being a part of the rags-to-riches-back-to-rags-again story, and watching your family going through pain and ultimately breaking apart, allows you to see a lot.

I will be the first to admit that this hit me hard.

I didn't take the divorce of my parents very well at all. This is really why I am telling my story because it helps you understand my mindset as a teenager, and how I would turn to my friends due to them being some kind of escape. It was my way for searching for those who would 'get me'.

The bitterness of a kid

When you are at a 'delicate' age and your parents split up, you can easily find yourself becoming resentful and make decisions that are disruptive to your life.

The "Why me?" and "Life sucks!" outlook can easily kick in, which then causes you to act differently to before.

Back then I looked at my parents divorcing as selfish in some ways, as I wasn't used to them putting their needs in front of ours. I didn't like the fact that they were turning our lives upside down and splitting the family up – just because they didn't love each other as much as they used to.

It's crazy to think this now, but back then I felt hard done by and I was thinking thoughts like "How could you do this to me?" A typical teenager's perspective I suppose, but at that age I saw things as being unfair.

This viewpoint of mine caused me to look for relationships and connections with people outside my family (possibly those who had been through the same kind of experience) so I started to hang out with my friends more and seek people who I could feel good with.

This is when things come full circle back to the topic of this chapter. It explains why I started to put more importance on being with my friends compared to putting any effort into my education or actively trying to start my racing career.

As soon as I passed my driving test, I still wanted to go racing... but if you were to look at how I spent my time, I would be spending 90 percent of it with my friends. So my racing endeavours didn't even get off the ground.

Once again, all this sounds crazy to me now and even hard to admit, but I truly believe that behaving this way was just my younger self trying to figure things out. It would ultimately lead me to where I am now. Thankfully.

A mother's wisdom

I was one of those teenagers you see parked up in McDonald's car parks late at night. We would be there virtually every night showing off our cheap modified hot hatchback cars and looking for something exciting to do that would occupy us in the moment.

We were all too young to own our own houses so we would park up anywhere that could potentially have something even remotely interesting happen. The camaraderie was strong between us all – but in terms of us making progress in life, well... our lives were effectively on pause.

My parents were becoming very concerned about my behaviour and how I was wasting my life. But instead of busting my backside about it too much, and causing even more distance between us, they came up with a cunning plan.

My mother knew how much I wanted to race and that the helplessness of not being able to afford it (or even knowing where to start in such a sport) would keep me on the streets. If so, things were not likely to end well for me.

So she, with my father's agreement, decided to raise the money for me so I could enrol in the top race school in the UK at that time. It was called the Jim Russell Race School and they had a course that I would often talk about.

Their plan was to help kick things off for me on the racing side in the hope that this would be the catalyst for getting my life in order. They knew I would jump at the chance of doing anything racing-related and this would hopefully grab my attention enough to put me on a different path in life.

I'm paraphrasing here but I remember my mother saying something like: "Look Enzo, you're in a rut right now and this won't play out well for you, but me and your dad want to help you get out of it. We are going to give you the chance to chase your dream."

I was sold immediately.

They went ahead and scraped the money together to enrol me into it; I think it was £2,500. They even sold a car in order to get the funding for this, so they were 'all in' at a time when they really didn't have the money.

As I look back at this now, my heart warms – because this was a pure example of how much parents will do for their children.

This took a lot of commitment to pull off because £2,500 was a lot of money for us back in 1994, but it was an ingenious move by my parents... and it worked. They gave me the gift of life by giving birth to me in the first place, then they gave me another gift of life by doing this.

You may be thinking: “So what, they enrolled you in a race school course.” But believe me, this was my actual turning point in life. I was heading down the road to pain until they did this.

I was over the moon. For the first time in my life I could see a bright future – and, just like what my parents did with the pizza shop, I could see a way for me to create my own success story. This was my opportunity and I was going to grab it with both hands.

It worked. My parents didn’t need to go down the route of banning me from hanging around with my friends. Instead they gave me something worth much more: a shot at pursuing something I loved even more.

This immediately shaped me, and my full focus was pointed towards becoming a race driver. I delivered pizzas, worked in a factory, worked as a race mechanic, attracted sponsors and did anything I could to gather up the money to race.

Since then, I have been able to have all kinds of different friends. But never have they distracted me from my goals or caused me to put my life on hold. Thanks Mom and Dad.

Could this approach work for you?

What my parents did was to give me something I truly wanted. This gave me a shot at starting a new life that was very aligned with my values and desires.

On top of this, they also hit home that my part of the deal was to give this chance my full effort; to pay them back through my dedication and to give it my all. All they wanted from me was to commit.

My belief up to that point was that "racing is not for people like me." And, due to me not having a clue where to start in motorsport, I chose to be a bum in life. That was until I saw my parents make sacrifices for that race school fee and show me it was actually possible. This changed my beliefs and created an outlook (Mental Matrix) that would change the direction of my life forever.

If you feel your child is in a similar position, ask yourself whether the tactic my parents used could inspire something that may work for you and your child in some way.

Maybe they too have lost their way due to losing hope or by having nothing meaningful to sink their teeth into. If so, feel free to deploy some kind of similar strategy that will grab their attention and change their outlook on life.

This may take some brainstorming, but if you know what drives your child or what gets them excited then you may just have the spark that's needed to fire them up. Add this to them understanding that all they have to do in return is put the work in, and they may just respond to this.

They may 'poo-poo' it to start with, but over time they may come around until they utter the words: "I'm ready."

Your driver and their friends

There are quite a few different challenges that parents have when it comes to their children, and the way that their friends are hampering their racing. Here are some examples:

- Drivers dropping their work ethic due to the time they spend with their friends
- Drivers seeming to be more interested in what their friends are doing, even while they are competing (partying, going to festivals, having fun elsewhere, etc)
- Drivers choosing friends who are 'no good' for them

- Drivers worrying too much about what their friends will think of them, which is affecting their performance in some way
- When the driver's friends come to the races it is distracting and is not helpful

You may be in a situation where you are paying for or assisting your child to race, but they are taking you for granted and not putting in the work – just because they want to spend all their time with their friends.

Maybe they are lying about them putting in the work when in fact they are hanging at their mates' houses.

If this is the case I cannot tell you what to do, but personally I would use good old 'Tough Love' and honesty.

If you hold the purse strings or if your child depends on you for their racing, yet they take advantage of you and do not meet you halfway with their commitment, I would simply pull the plug. They may need a harsh wake-up call – and a reminder about how they are being rude by expecting you to pay for things when they cannot be bothered to approach it in the required way.

Your driver has to learn just how much commitment this sport requires. In fact, they need to fully understand how much dedication it takes to succeed at anything in life. Racing provides drivers with many life skills, and this topic is just one of those.

The general tough love rule is: They do not get to go racing or get another penny from you unless they commit and pull their weight.

This may be difficult to do, but you cannot let your driver take advantage of you. It is downright disrespectful for a driver to expect others to help them race with no return benefit. If they are paying for their own racing then fair enough, they can have fun with friends. But if a sponsor or you are creating the opportunity, they must meet certain requirements and there will be duties attached to this.

That's life.

A parent's role

It's the parent's role to be the disciplinarian, set the standards of behaviour and give a child the life lessons/skills needed so they can survive once the parent is no longer here.

As you can tell, I am quite passionate about this. This is because I see so many drivers walking all over their parents. The parents want to keep their Little Johnny happy so they bend over backwards to keep their child happy... but in doing so the child often takes advantage of things and treats their parents like dirt.

I don't want parents to stand for this. The parent must be the authoritative figure and they must always have the final say.

Obviously this role changes somewhat as the child becomes an adult and goes on to have children themselves. But for the purpose of this book, where most of the drivers are not at that stage of their lives, the parents must continue to help steer the ship (if needed).

Girlfriends and boyfriends

When it comes to the friends of your driver, things can be straightforward. You can freely express your feelings about their friends or how you want your driver to focus more. They will often take it as you nagging, but it isn't such a hard conversation to have with your child.

However, when it comes to intimate relationships your driver has, things can become more complex because you are dealing with the heart strings here.

Without banging on about my own life, I remember having a girlfriend that my family and friends were not happy with. We went out for quite a long time but due to friends and family not agreeing with the relationship, I chose to distance myself from them all and I spent most of my time with the girlfriend instead.

Friends and family used to ask things like: "What has happened to Enzo?"

Due to nobody really liking her or seeing us as a good fit, I started to spend less time with my friends and family. I distanced myself because I believed they just didn't understand – and due to my love for her, I blindly put her first.

Once again I had made personal decisions that would not serve me and they completely screwed up my priorities. On this occasion it actually caused me to work even harder on my racing but it still wasn't the correct thing to do.

The crazy thing? It wasn't even a great relationship. We would argue a lot. I somehow believed I was happy and I bent over backwards to make it work, but the whole thing was dysfunctional.

I needed my head read.

It's embarrassing to think about it now but there was even a time, while I was racing at Snetterton, when we were arguing in the collection area right before a race. It ended up with her slamming the race car door as I was about to drive onto the grid.

What a douche I was. I would never accept this if one of my drivers was going through this, yet I allowed it to happen.

After about six years I finally came to my senses, and I have since made much better decisions when it comes to relationships. But this goes to show how relationships can mess us up and totally disrupt things – especially when you are still fairly young and finding your feet.

This is obviously something you do not want to happen to your driver, because being with someone who is causing complications and harmfully distracting your driver can be detrimental to their racing, to their relationship with you and to their life in general.

We are not in control anymore

Parents have a tough time with this subject, and rightly so, because you are the person who cares most about your child and only wants the best for them. Yet you are the person they listen to the least when it comes to their relationships.

For a parent it's like tightrope walking when it comes to handling this area.

Your driver may well be in a relationship that is not necessarily good for them, but as a parent you have to tread carefully because one wrong move and they could distance themselves from you.

This is super-frustrating because you can see what is going on, you can read people well and it is easy for you to predict how things will likely turn out.

This is scary because when it comes to intimate relationships your child will become somewhat brainwashed by their partner. And let's be real here: this is a real life decision that can affect things because they could end up getting pregnant. If so, things get even more complex.

So this is all a big worry. I don't need to tell you that.

Be there

Please remember that as I talk about this topic, I am just suggesting things that may give you food for thought. I am not telling you what to actually do because it is not my place to do so, and I do not know the intricacies of your situation.

Having said that, from what I have seen parents do in the past, what has proven most effective overall is when the objective parent remains supportive. That means being there for your child no matter what – and even though they may be in a relationship with someone that you do not agree with, it's often best to be open to that and not outwardly object too much.

It's a little bit like the saying: 'Keep your friends close but your enemies closer'. If we take that philosophy and apply it to your child's relationships, it means that instead of causing friction by objecting too much to their relationship – causing a disconnect between you and your child – it's often better to bite your tongue so you can remain close to the situation.

I personally think it is okay to voice your concern in a calm way, especially at the beginning of the relationship when they are not too attached to this new person yet. But if your concern becomes too loud, intrusive and persistent over time, expect your child to reduce communication with you.

A relationship is exciting to them; it's what they want and it gets their juices flowing. If you object too much when they are going through this, they will just see you as being the parent who 'doesn't understand' and you end up being someone they can no longer connect with.

Add all of this to your child wanting to prove to you that they can now make their own decisions in life – and wanting to show you they no longer need to be told what to do – and you have the perfect storm if this isn't handled correctly.

That's why I think that by showing them (even though you may have concerns) that you are willing to be accommodating to their partner and allow them to spend time with each other, things will run much smoother. This means you can actually have a little more control over the situation.

If you choose to do this, offer to involve the partner in family trips and get-togethers, let them hang out at home and keep yourself as part of the relationship.

What I have seen work is when the parent is present or close by – and not causing friction, even though they are not happy with the person their child has chosen.

This is stupidly hard to do but this is often the best option. Eventually the driver comes round to realising things on their own and the relationship fizzles out...

A parent's mental tactics

At the end of the day there is little you can do about the person your child chooses to get involved with because they have to figure things out for themselves. But I am sure there are certain tactics that you know of, and have used in the past, that get your point across.

I mean this in a nice way.

You will already know what buttons to push and what works for your child when you are trying to get them to see things in a certain way. Parents are masters at this, and even though it gets harder as they get older I am sure that you can figure out ways of subliminally communicating things to them so they can come up with their own healthy conclusions.

It's a little bit like what my mother did when she raised the money for me to go to the race school. She gave up on telling me that my choice of friends and the way I was spending my life was not good for me. Instead she played the mental game and offered me something I wanted more.

I'm not saying you can do this when it comes to relationships, but still this was my mother knowing my values and helping me figure things out.

It wasn't until many years later that I realised the mental game she pulled off right there... but I am so grateful that she did.

Summary

It's impossible for me to give you specifics on this. But you will have certain cards that you can play, ethically, that will help your child come to terms with things quicker and maybe help them see they can do better when it comes to who they are spending time with.

Your child is a human, which means they are required to make their own mistakes when it comes to their relationships. So my overriding advice here is to be there for them no matter what... and help them come to their own conclusions.

This may take time and patience but life has its own path and way of playing things out. Protecting your child from the pain life can bestow upon them is what parents feel they are here for; you want to protect your children, but there are some things they have to learn for themselves.

Relationships fall into that category, so just be there for them no matter what. Show your love for them and let them know you are always there for them.

PART 3:
CAREER ADVICE

CHAPTER 14
CHOOSING THE CORRECT CAREER PATH

Welcome to Part 3 of the book, where we will turn our attention to the career aspects and challenges you and your driver may face on your racing journey. And where better to start off than by addressing career paths?

The overall objective when designing any driver's career path is quite obvious: we simply want to choose a route that gives them the best chance of achieving a professional career.

That doesn't sound too difficult.

Well, it may sound simple... but that doesn't mean it's easy. Because when you are in charge of making career decisions for a driver, you must make sure you put them in the right place at the right time – ideally in championships that are aligned with their long term goal and that will help them showcase their talent.

You will have heard of many drivers who had the talent to reach the pinnacle of the sport, only for their attempts to fail. That was because they were either in the wrong place at the wrong time or they made incorrect career decisions as they climbed the racing ladder.

Many drivers trip up in this way. This is partially due to these drivers or their family receiving misguided advice from people in the industry who put their own agendas first.

It is super-important that a driver's advisors genuinely have the driver's interest at the forefront of their mind when choosing the next championship to run in – and when designing the overall plan.

They also need to understand their driver. They need to be fully aware of their driver's strengths and weaknesses so that the driver can be positioned in a series and a team that will help them get the results they need.

It's like this in the sport of boxing too. The opponents of a boxer are hand-picked and chosen for a reason. They cannot afford to take a loss early on so the promoters must put their fighter in the ring with someone who has a style that complements them.

We can take a similar approach when it comes to a race driver's career path.

This doesn't mean we hide them from tough competition; it just means we need to give them the best chance possible so we can build their brand and their stock value in the sport.

Emotions can rule us

In life we often allow our emotions to influence our decisions – and these decisions often take us further away from what we actually want long term.

This is not just in our careers, we do it on a daily basis. It's like having that chocolate bar even though we are trying to lose weight, or calling up your ex-partner after having too many alcoholic drinks.

Parents and drivers can easily get carried away – or get talked into making career choices which may seem exciting initially, but often turn into the very reasons why the driver's career comes to a premature end.

Logic often gets ignored when we are emotionally invested in something, so please be careful of this.

You will see drivers entering championships that are either not suited for their current skill level, or drivers taking a certain route just because it's fashionable to do so. I see more drivers making these kinds of errors than I see drivers getting things right.

So the first word of advice I have on this topic is that when you are making decisions for what and where your driver should race next season, you must distance yourself from making any knee-jerk emotional choices and be very calculated about things.

A lot of this will come down to your knowledge of the industry and being self-aware enough to know the exact skill level of your young racer.

The business perspective

If we look at this in business terms and translate it all in a way that relates to the business world, you can view a driver as a product. When selling a product or trying to get investment for its creation, you need to:

1. Fully understand what the product does well (and what it doesn't do well)
2. Know how good it is compared to other products out there (the competition)
3. Improve the product if it isn't at the level of the competition

4. Position the product in the market where it will sell; somewhere that will help you showcase it so it can stand out and where people will see the value in buying it

If you look at drivers in a similar way – even though this is your child we are talking about – you are much more likely to make the best decision for them.

A grey area

It's a very grey area to talk about career decisions in a book like this, because each driver has their own unique situation so there isn't a 'one answer fits all' here.

If you really want to make the right decision for any given driver then you have to take their financial situation, political restrictions/advantages, business relationships, current reputation, racing record, skill level, goals, team selection – and, dare I say it, their age – all into account when deciding what route is best for them.

On top of this, even though the path you want to take may be very obvious when you start out, due to the above factors and what actually happens over the years, you will experience many twists and turns that may force your hand a certain way. Even destiny will play a part in this. This is where the waters muddy and things are not always clear.

However, I still want to give you some advice here because I might touch upon something that will be relevant to you.

The 30-second career path question

If somebody was to ask me for advice on what their next career move should be and they wanted a quick answer, I would start off by asking them these four questions:

1. What's your long term goal?
2. What results and speed have you shown up to now?

3. How much budget (money or sponsorship) do you have access to?
4. How old are you?

These questions will provide fact-based answers that are essential to know before you can advise a driver on possible options. Once you know these facts, things become a lot clearer.

To give you a very straightforward example, if the driver answered my four questions with...

1. I want to get to F1
2. I have just won the European Karting Championship
3. We have access to $5million to spend on our racing over the next 4 years
4. I am 14 years old

...then you don't need to be a genius to answer this, right?

Given the current structure of the F1 ladder system, I would tell them to do a mainstream Formula 4 championship for a year or two. Then, depending on their results, skill level and offers from race teams, they would either go to Formula Regional or the FIA F3 championship.

Once they were competing well in F3, they would then go to F2. Then if their results were impressive enough, and if they gathered sponsors or got the backing from an F1 junior team along the way, they would stand a chance of getting into F1.

If not, but they still got to a high level in single-seaters, they could shift over to the IndyCar or World Endurance routes.

Again, all obvious stuff.

This is the kind of path many drivers have taken in the past, and the current superlicence structure virtually dictates that drivers must go this way if they want to get to F1.

You can also approach things by competing in other championships, like the ones on the Road To Indy programme. But for the best chance (if the driver has the finance and the speed) you should compete within the F4, F3, F2, F1 ladder – not forgetting Formula Regional if needed.

By the way, I fully appreciate your driver may well not be in the privileged situation to even entertain thoughts about the route to F1.

Your driver may dream of F1 but their age, financial situation and results simply do not make the normal route possible.

If this is the case, we have to get creative. But first you still need to be very clear on the four questions I originally asked. From there you can start to make a plan.

F1 is one of the only championships that seems to have such a strict path to it. But when it comes to most of the other top tier championships, such as IndyCar, World Endurance Championship, DTM and NASCAR, as a driver you can reach these championships in numerous ways.

Some obscure career paths

For a great example of an out-of-the-ordinary career path, look no further than Scott McLaughlin. Here is someone who, aged 27, became a full-time IndyCar driver in 2001 for one of the best teams around: Team Penske.

If you didn't know his racing history and you saw him competing in IndyCar, you would think he must have taken the normal route. This may have included series like USF2000, Indy Pro 2000 and/or Indy Lights. Or maybe that he raced in the formula categories in Europe.

But he didn't. Instead Scott went directly from the Supercars championship in Australia.

Prior to joining IndyCar, he hadn't raced a formula car since his first year of car racing (Formula Ford 1600) back in 2010.

We hardly ever see drivers go from a touring car championship to something like IndyCar. That's an amazing career shift.

He did well too. He was awarded Rookie Of The Year in 2021 – and within five months of picking up that Rookie trophy he won his first IndyCar race in the 2022 season.

That's impressive for more than one reason. First for having the confidence to make such an unusual career path switch and second for being competitive so quickly.

This backs up a certain belief of mine; I have always reckoned that if you are a truly good driver, you can drive anything.

Another example of an obscure path to the top that comes to mind is Allan McNish and his route to F1. Unlike Scott, Allan was actually a driver who spent most of his earlier career racing formula cars. He had some success in British F3 in 1989 but after that he barely won any races until he switched to sportscar racing in 1995.

His mind was fully settled on an endurance career. But little did he know that seven years later, in 2002, at the age of 32, he would make his F1 debut. He did the whole season with Toyota and he actually managed to finish P7 in only his second race in F1.

Many of the cars didn't finish that race but still, this is another good example of how obscure some of motorsport's career paths have been.

With eSports becoming more important now, I envisage us seeing even more interesting career paths. That's because we will hopefully develop scholarships that will help drivers go from their bedroom to real life racing.

We saw how successful this route could be with Jann Mardenborough. Just three years after winning the PlayStation GT Academy competition, he was racing in the top F3 championship – and he has had a pretty impressive racing career considering how he started.

Who would have thought you could go from entering an online competition using Gran Turismo as its base to creating a real racing career like that?!?

We need more of these competitions.

I could keep listing these obscure paths to the top, but I think you get the idea. My point here is that you may need to think outside the box if your driver doesn't have either the results or the finances to climb the 'normal' ladder system.

Many other drivers have also shown that if they just keep improving and winning in different categories, you never know what opportunities will present themselves in the future. When Plan A doesn't go as you wanted, there is always a Plan B, C, D and so on.

If you remain in the game, you never know what will come up.

The costs of championships

It is super-hard to give you precise figures on how much it costs to get a shot at reaching the top championships in the world. That's because it depends on what career path is used, what results the driver gets, or if they get backing and cheaper race deals. But to give you a very basic understanding of the market value for each main route, here is my attempt (in Euros).

F1 = €7.4 million – F4, F3 and F2 (2 years in each)

IndyCar = €3.8 million – USF2000, Indy Pro and Indy Lights (2 years in each)

World Endurance Championship = €2.9 million – GT, LMP3, LMP2

NASCAR = €11 million – using top teams in ARCA, Trucks and Xfinity

Again, please understand these figures are very dependent on your situation, because some drivers have paid way less than these prices. Having said that, some drivers (who did more years in certain categories or didn't manage to get cheaper deals with teams) paid way more than these figures.

For example, on the World Endurance Championship career path, a driver may have paid their way up to F2, then realised they couldn't make the jump to F1. So instead they paid for a season in LMP2 before securing a professional contract.

That would mean this driver had spent approximately €8.4million in order for themselves to get into a paid driver role.

This may not be a great return on investment. But I do believe that if you want to get the attention of the manufacturers and you have the money to do so, going as high up the single-seater ladder as possible does often help.

Manufacturers understand that a top ten F2 or F3 driver is often quick in anything they drive, especially prototypes.

This is always something to consider but I have found that once a driver has a winning record at the F3 level, with the right management they are looking good for achieving a professional career. F3 has always been a level where the sport starts to take drivers seriously.

This may be something to keep in mind.

Silly numbers

If these stupidly high numbers are scaring the hell out of you then... welcome to motorsport! It's getting crazy out here.

In all honesty though, your racing doesn't have to cost this much. You can race nationally at a fairly high level for under €250k per year.

In Europe we have British GT, the DTM Trophy or any of the national Porsche Carrera championships which are more cost effective. If you do well there you can still grab the attention of manufacturers.

Racing in these championships may not be your first choice but if done correctly with the right kind of driver, they can create a very impressive racing career.

Questions to keep you on track

It can be quite pressured when you are the person who is deciding on the best route for your driver, but you should know it might not be as black and white as you may think.

Very often there isn't a completely right or wrong answer because things change in the industry. And as I mentioned earlier, drivers who are worthy of making a career in this sport (those who are winning) often get picked up by professional teams no matter what championship they are in.

Hindsight is an amazing thing when it comes to career and life decisions, so in some ways you can only go by what you know now and get the driver to work their tail off to stand out or win. Then what will be, will be.

To help make the decision process easier, I suggest you should answer these questions:

1. What championships offer a possible route upward?
2. What championships can my driver do well in?

3. What is possible to afford?
4. Which championship can we enter with a competitive team/car?
5. What are the goals for next year (learning or winning)?

Once you answer these questions, you can start to narrow down what would be the best series for next season and come up with a shortlist.

Next you can talk with the teams within those championships to gauge their interest and see what budgets they can offer you, then take things from there.

You also may need to remind yourself of the above questions as time goes by so you can keep on track and not allow other people to distract you from what matters.

Sometimes it's better to prioritise your driver's short term goals over their long term ones. Yes, it is great for them to use the championship with long term goals in mind – but if they are ready to win, then put them in a situation where they can win next year.

However, if they are not ready to win just yet – and they need to be in an environment where they can comfortably improve at their own pace – I recommend putting them in a championship and a team that will help them learn the basics and get things polished before going for the bigger series.

If the driver isn't ready to shine in the bigger series, it is often better to keep them off the radar a little longer and get them winning at the lower level first. Reputation is everything in this sport, and you need the industry to value your driver, so you want them to be ready for when they step up.

As I mentioned earlier, this is where logic and common sense needs to be listened to – rather than emotions.

If a driver is naturally quick already and they can handle jumping up quickly, then by all means do it. It worked well for

Max Verstappen and Kimi Raikkonen (who were both in F1 in only their second year of car racing) but you must have the evidence that this is the case before jumping up.

I suggest that you test your driver in the bigger car first before making any final decisions.

What I am trying to say here is that the best career path is one that is matched to:

1. The driver's goals
2. The driver's available finances
3. The driver's ability/skill/speed

If you get clear on all these aspects and put them in a series that aligns with them, you are likely to choose the best championship for them. Then just repeat this each year until things become clear.

Next we will talk about race team selection, an important area that goes hand-in-hand with a driver's career path choice... and may actually dictate what championship you choose.

Advice from others

You can ask other people for their opinions in reference to the best career path to take, but be very careful who you trust.

Race teams, other parents, coaches and even your own manager may have ulterior motives and their own reasons for what they advise you to do – which means they may see things from their own perspective or personal gain.

You need to put your driver first here, so by all means gather up the advice others give you. But remember to ask yourself all the questions that I have put to you in this chapter so you and your driver can make an educated decision and have the final say.

CHAPTER 15
CHOOSING A RACE TEAM

It goes without saying that race team selection plays a major role in a driver's career – and it can be another make-or-break decision that parents, drivers and managers have to make each year.

You can put a fast driver in a top championship but if they are in a team that is uncompetitive or underperforming, or if the team is even mistreating the driver, the wheels can easily fall off the career wagon.

The obvious choice when selecting a team is to go for the team that had the best results the previous season.

Well... not always.

I say this because once again it depends on multiple factors. As you can tell and as you may have already found out, decisions in motorsport are hardly ever straightforward.

When it comes to team selection, things don't just depend on the driver's goals and the team's past performance. We also need to consider the driver's reputation in the paddock, past results, available budget and even the personal relationships the driver or their management may have with these top teams.

You must also look into what package a team can offer you in terms of the machinery and staff your driver will get. Is it going to be a competitive car with a good engineer and mechanic, or will you get the trainee engineer with a car that has never finished in the top 10? These are factors that need to be found out first.

Simply calling up the current series champions and expecting to get the top package is a common mistake made by drivers. So be careful here because some teams will tell you what you want to hear in the early stages... but then go against their own promises once the contract is signed.

The timing needs to be right for the driver too. If they are in their first year of racing and not quite up to speed yet, thrusting them into a top team before they are ready to showcase their level can be detrimental to the driver's reputation in the paddock – and their own confidence.

If you are in a top team, everybody expects your driver to win. If they are not winning, but their teammates are, your driver's reputation will be massively harmed.

If they need to be with a team that will help them master the fundamentals in year one – and do it more out of the spotlight – so be it. They can then approach the top teams in year two.

In taking this approach you not only help your driver focus on what's important (improving) but it helps with team negotiations the following year. You obviously stand a much better chance of getting a better deal and a better package if your driver has shown promise beforehand.

It's better to be the driver who progressed during the season with a second-rate team, than a driver who underachieved in a top team.

Obviously this is dependent on your driver's current level. If they are showing good speed in testing, get them into a top team with a good package included in that deal.

Shared objectives

Before I go too deep here, I want to give an overview of what the driver's and the team's objectives are. We can then work backwards to understand how things play out in reality so you can make the right decisions.

You will be happy to know that drivers and teams have similar goals. Put very simply, they both want to win – and they want to earn money doing it.

They both have their racing and financial dreams to fulfil, and these factors will be at the forefront of their minds when making decisions for the coming season.

In saying that, even though the objectives of each party are identical, they may have different short term priorities. So their ways of going about things can differ quite a lot.

Teams want to win in order to improve their brand so they can attract good drivers and have a successful business. A team also needs to get the money in, year on year, so they can keep the lights on, pay their staff, innovate and prepare the cars as best they can.

Drivers also need to win to improve their brand. But this is so they can further their career, please their sponsors and eventually help themselves secure future contracts that will allow them to earn money while they live their passion.

The objectives are the same, but the priorities are slightly different. Teams need the money now, whereas drivers are willing to pay to race for many years before they receive their first pay cheque.

This slight difference in priorities makes for an interesting situation: the team needs immediate cash flow, but a driver needs immediate results.

It may sound like a match made in heaven... but in reality it leads both teams and drivers to make some very short-sighted decisions.

Short term relationship

Unlike most business arrangements in other industries and sports, when it comes to the team/driver relationship, things are very short-lived.

The driver will look at a racing team as a temporary stepping stone towards their long term goals, and a race team will look upon a driver in a similar way.

A driver wants to use a team's expertise in order to help them win next season, but after that they may well choose a different team when they want to improve their results or move up a category.

The team views the driver as someone who can help them pay their bills in that given year. Even though they sometimes don't like it, teams well know – and accept – that a driver may only be with them for a single season before joining another team.

So both parties are kind of using each other in the current time so they can both keep on track with their individual North Star Goals.

It's like having an unspoken arrangement where both parties think to themselves "You give me what I want, I will give you what you want, and we then go our separate ways."

It's never said this way, but that's the way things are set up and generally accepted. It's only when you become a professional driver with a professional contract that the team and the driver start to think more long term together.

Teams would like to keep their drivers within their stable for multiple years because they build up relationships and drivers know some of their secrets. But they are fully aware it isn't always possible to do this.

This short term viewpoint can mean some teams take advantage of their drivers. They know they will only be with them for a year or so, so they'd better extract as much money from them as they can while they have them.

Not every team is like this, of course, but it still has to be considered when dealing with teams, because not all of them work to the same priorities or with the same morals that you do.

If you ever get a team that no longer talks to you because you left them at the end of the season, that's their problem not yours. They should know drivers move on and team bosses should know better than to take it personally.

If they are pissed at you leaving, it's probably because they are upset to be losing the income they were relying on next season. Again, that is not your problem. You and your driver must come first.

Teams playing budget games

As I have already alluded to, there is a lot more to selecting the right team for your driver than just putting them with a top team.

To understand what I mean, we need to remember this sport is a business. A successful team is only successful because they get the best drivers, best engineers and best equipment – and usually they charge the most money in order to do all this.

The fastest drivers out there often do not have the most money. So, for a top team to attract such drivers, they often need to offer these quick drivers a very competitive deal.

This in turn means the team may charge their other drivers more money to help them do this.

For example, if a team has to spend $3 million in order to run their three-car team, you would think the logical thing to do would be to charge all three drivers $1 million each.

In reality though, if the team wants to sign a certain driver due to their speed – but that particular driver doesn't have much money behind them – they may think tactfully here and overcharge the other two drivers so they can offer the fast driver a tempting deal.

They may charge the other two drivers $1.25 million each, and only charge the fast driver $500,000.

This is a classic example of the team looking after their interests first. It makes sense and you can't blame a team for doing this because they need to do what they can to win. But it's not nice if you are the driver paying more.

Obviously it doesn't always work this way, but you mustn't lose sight of this. If your driver hasn't proven themselves yet via their results, or they are a rookie to the series, they will most likely be one of the drivers in the team who are paying the most money.

What's more, they might not be getting the preferential treatment in terms of what team staff are allocated to your driver's car. I am not saying every team will do this, but it is very common.

Remember that it's business, it's not personal.

It is also another reason why I keep banging on about getting your driver into a situation or a series where they can win. Either that or you make sure you get the coaching assistance to help your driver win... because **results are seriously important**.

This is not just for the driver's overall brand and career; previous results are very important when it comes to negotiating with new teams.

Anyway, back to the top teams...

The good things about joining a top team in a respected championship are:

1. They will have a good understanding of the car, tyres and how to win
2. They will usually have a good driver preparation procedure in place
3. You have a lot of data from previous drivers in the team that can help your driver advance
4. The cars are usually prepared well and they have good reliability
5. They will usually have well-qualified staff and they will be organised
6. They usually have good contacts in the sport to help your driver advance after the season

The 'not so good' things about top teams:

1. If your driver is not up to standard, they will be exposed. With top teams, you must win or fight for wins. No excuses
2. They normally cost more than other teams
3. Sometimes they will tell you how to drive and presume they know more than you (but that isn't always a bad thing)
4. It can often turn into a bidding war between other parents (budget-wise)

As you can see, there are not many negatives for joining a successful team. But just make sure that your driver is ready to shine, that you are not seriously over-paying for the drive and that your driver gets a good crew working with them on their car for that season.

What to find out about a team

There are many things you need to be aware of when deciding who to run with. Some things you can ask face-to-face when you meet them while some things can be researched.

Here is quite an extensive list of things you can find out before signing with a team:

1. What have their previous results been like?
2. What do their previous drivers say about them? (Prepare for some unhappy previous drivers no matter who the team is...)
3. How professional do they look?
4. How clean and prepared do the cars look at race weekends?
5. How organised and clean is the workshop/truck/staff uniform?
6. What chassis will you have and what is its history?
7. Who will be working on the car – engineer, mechanics, etc?
8. How good is the team boss at their job?
9. What does the budget cover – accommodation, insurance, minor work on the car, etc?
10. How many test days does your contract include?
11. How many tyres per test day do you get?
12. What is the payment schedule like in the contract, and are you happy with it?
13. What sponsorship space do you get on the car, race suit, truck, etc?
14. Is there any team hospitality for sponsors, guests and family?

15. Is there any sponsorship assistance – or any chance of subsidising the drive through their current sponsors?
16. How many race passes do you get included?
17. What is the damage excess?
18. How do the preparation days at the workshop work?
19. Who will the teammates be?
20. How often are things replaced on the car – brakes, engine rebuild, chassis checked, etc?
21. What is the financial health of the team?
22. What other championships do they race in, and will joining them help you advance with them?

Whether you ask these questions yourself or your manager does, they are all good to know and they will give you a good idea of whether this is the right team for you.

If you do have a manager, this is where they earn their money. The manager is the person who must ensure all of this is clear and that you get the best deal/package possible. They must also get the team to guarantee your driver will receive the same treatment and service, if not better, than their teammates.

Ask around

When we are deciding which holiday package to choose or which hotel to stay in, most of us check out their reviews before booking. Everyone does it: we look at the star rating and comments left by previous customers.

I often allow these reviews to influence my decision when I'm looking for a holiday. In fact, I do this with pretty much everything I buy.

We do not yet have such a reviewing system for race teams, but there are plenty of people in the paddock who can shine some light on which teams are good (and not so good) to run with in your championship. So never be afraid to ask.

Yes, there will be some people who have had a bad experience with a good team, where things just didn't work out. But if you ask around enough, you can get a good read from all the comments you hear. Then you can decide whether or not to approach certain teams.

Past drivers, managers, coaches, race engineers and mechanics can all be fairly reliable people to ask – as long as they have no affiliation, personal gain or hang-ups related to the particular teams you are enquiring about.

Once you have a shortlist of teams you are happy with, it's time to speak to each one. Contact them directly and, if you like what you hear, visit their workshop and take things from there.

It's also a good idea to do a test with your preferred team or teams, so you can see what they are all about and how they work with your driver.

Contract time

Once you have selected which team (or final couple of teams) you wish to join, the next step is to get them to provide you with a driver contract. This is the time to put on your legal hat – and think more with your mind than your heart.

The contract will state exactly what the team will provide you and your driver with, and it will list out the terms for providing such a service.

That's all good, but make sure they clearly state that they will provide your driver with a competitive car... and that they are clear on all aspects relating to their own performance and service.

I say this because you have to put out as many potential fires as possible at this early stage. A team that may look good upfront still has the potential to underperform and do things that are not helpful for your driver. A contract will hold a team legally accountable for such things and ensure they deliver the service they are selling to you.

As you climb the racing ladder, the price tag also climbs. So things often have to be done legally to give you or your sponsors reassurance that your money will be spent correctly – and everything will be accounted for.

You need the team to spell out everything they are providing you (number of test days and tyres, which personnel are working with your driver, equipment, insurance details, level of preparation, etc) so you have something concrete to refer to should you need it later on.

Also make sure you are comfortable with the payment structure. It is normal for teams to front-load the payments you make, so for example if you were paying $100,000 for the season, the payment structure may look something like this:

- $35,000 on signing contract
- $15,000 on month 2
- $15,000 on month 3
- $15,000 on month 4
- $10,000 on month 5
- $10,000 on month 6

Teams structure it like this because they have big outlays at the beginning of the season (registration fees, car rebuild, employing staff to work prior to the season, new equipment, new truck, etc). They also want to make sure you and your driver are committed.

It's always a risk for a team when they sign a new driver. They have to trust that the driver has the money to complete the season – or enough money put away should the driver leave prematurely.

Incidents and force majeure

It is always a good idea to ensure your team contract has clauses that cover unfortunate circumstances – such as what happens if...

- Your driver gets injured
- The team cannot get to an event for some reason (truck breaking down, incident at the workshop, etc)
- You and your driver are unhappy with the performance or service of the team
- You have to make payments later than scheduled
- The team get disqualified from a race or championship
- The team make a mistake that damages the car or causes it to breakdown/fail on track

There are plenty of things that can go wrong in any given season, so take the time to ensure they are covered in the contract. Alternatively, add some clauses if required.

Talking of unfortunate circumstances, you also want to make sure you have a force majeure clause that covers more global incidents that can affect everyone in the championship.

To give you an example, when the Imola F1 race event was cancelled due to flooding in 2023, all the F2 and F3 race teams who were also racing that weekend had to communicate to their drivers what their protocol was for when such an incident happens.

Due to the race weekend being called off so close to the event itself (the Wednesday before) the teams couldn't simply give the drivers their money back for that weekend – because the team staff and trucks were already there, so they had incurred a lot of the normal costs.

The team had paid for all the logistics, hotel rooms that couldn't be cancelled, food for the event, staff for their time, and so on. It wasn't the team's fault that the race didn't go ahead... so they had done everything they were contractually obliged to do. Even so, the drivers were also not at fault. So this is a classic force majeure situation.

That means you have to make sure such an incident is covered in your contract. These things don't happen every year, but they do happen.

The contract phase shouldn't be rushed. Check everything and get legal assistance if required – because you want to cover all the bases and make sure both you and the team enter into the agreement in the right way.

Summary

When it comes to a race team you just want one that will have a proven track record for what you are looking for (results, training, work ethic, etc) and one that people say good things about around the paddock.

Most of the time you get what you pay for when it comes to a team, but make sure you are always getting the biggest bang for your buck.

If your driver needs time to learn the ropes and is not yet up to speed, put them with a team that teaches drivers well and looks after them. However, if your driver is 'ready to pop' and to show what they are made of, go for the most successful teams that will provide you with a competitive package.

You must know exactly what is included in the contract, then get the contract checked by a legal professional with motorsport experience and take things from there.

Get everything down in writing when it comes to communications with the team. Especially if the conversation has anything to do with money or the service they are providing. You literally have to talk to teams as if you have a lawyer looking over your shoulder, just in case things need to go down the legal route one day.

Every driver experiences situations where a team has not fulfilled their contractual obligations or they are not performing as stated. So as the parent, keep things formal and very clear. This way everyone knows where they stand and that they must behave.

You can change many things in the initial contract that a team issues you with, so go through it fully. Make sure you are 100 percent happy with the terms, the payment schedule, their duties and all eventualities that may occur throughout the season.

Unless you have to, do not rush the contract exchange period. I'd rather you were thorough before signing, than be regretful afterwards.

CHAPTER 16
DO WE NEED A MANAGER?

"Enzo, do you think we need a manager?"

This is a question that I get a lot – and rightly so, because as you walk the paddocks you will see that many drivers have a manager of some sort. So you can't help but wonder if that is something you need to help your child's career.

Within this chapter I am going to attempt to answer this question for you, or at the very least give you a few words of advice that will help you come to your own conclusions.

Navigating the minefield

More often than not, if you are a parent of a race driver there is a good chance that this is your first time in the sport. This can be a daunting experience.

I often refer to the world of motorsport as being a minefield because in many ways it is. At any moment the drivers, teams or parents can step in the wrong direction... and before they know it they are walking into a world of pain.

On any given day things can be going almost too well, only for things to fall apart the next.

As drivers attempt to win a championship or create a career, they are required to make constant decisions that all seem to have consequences attached to them. This can often cause drivers to hesitate, or be bullied into doing things that hamper them long term.

As I mentioned in chapter one, if you are actively assisting your driver with their racing, you have a big responsibility. Being able to make the correct moves (off track) at the right times will play a big part in their career.

I also refer to motorsport as a minefield because it's not only your decisions that can blow up in your face. The people who work within the sport can either mislead you or drain you of your resources just to meet their own objectives.

Don't get me wrong: there are some genuine team owners, managers and others in motorsport. But sometimes it can feel as though they are few and far between.

In some ways racing paddocks are like exhibition shows. You can be walking through, minding your own business, yet still you get pestered by exhibitors who are constantly trying to pull you into their stand so they can pitch their product or service to you.

They spend very little time thinking about your goals and they are far more interested in making a sale. Racing paddocks are often like this.

So when you get people like yourself, who are entering the sport for genuine sporting reasons, who are passionate about their child's racing career and looking for opportunities, the people who work in the industry (exhibitors) see you as potential income.

This interesting dynamic can cause parents to fall for some of the oldest tricks in the book; year after year you can see people getting lured into the same old traps.

When it comes to choosing the right team, the best championship, what to include in contracts, the career path and the correct kind of training, these areas all offer yet another chance for you to get ripped off.

This is why so many drivers and families start to think about employing a manager, especially once the driver gets to a level where it looks like a racing career might be possible. Then it leads to them asking the very question that started this chapter off.

The different types of management and their duties

If you have already scoured the internet looking for some kind of career assistance, you will have found there are many different types of management companies out there. So it can be very confusing to understand which is best for you and who will be a good, trustworthy fit.

To help you categorise them I have split the different types of management services out there into four categories. This is a very unofficial way of categorising them, but I think it's the best way to make sense of things.

1 - Management agencies

This type of management company takes care of every area of a driver's career, both in and out of the car. But their primary focus is a driver's career and all the related business aspects.

They do help drivers improve on the performance side – but usually they outsource the driver coaching, physical training, mental training, etc, to specialists outside their own company.

They charge a high retainer for their services but they will have the proven track record and the know-how for getting drivers to the pinnacle of motorsport.

Their main duties are to:

- Create a favourable career path for the driver
- Source available race seats
- Negotiate with race teams to provide you with a competitive package
- Deal with team and sponsorship contracts
- Ensure that race teams deliver on their contractual obligations
- Find opportunities with professional teams, driver programmes and manufacturers when the driver is ready
- Assist with commercial/sponsorship negotiations and support
- Offer motorsport legal advice
- Help with the driver's branding, design work, social media and overall PR

If required, they will also put in place the trainers and coaches who will help the driver improve, though this may well be an added extra.

A good management agency will know the industry well, they will have many contacts who can offer opportunities, they will have a proven track record, they will have a thorough understanding of sports law and of drawing up/reviewing contracts. They will also be very organised so each client of theirs gets the required attention.

As I write this, depending on what is included and how good the agency is, the fees for hiring such a company will range from £40,000 to £110,000 per year.

This may sound like a lot of extra money to pay out. But in my experience, if you are shooting for a professional career these agencies will not only provide you serious value, but long term they will save you more money than what it costs to hire them.

For example, they will usually be able to get race seats cheaper than if you called the race teams directly yourself. They will save you making expensive mistakes, they will offer you opportunities that probably wouldn't have been offered to you alone and they take a lot of the pressure off you as a parent because they put out the fires.

These agencies pretty much take care of everything and they work tirelessly not only to protect their drivers but to give them the best possible shot at becoming a professional race driver.

If the cost for a manager is near the six-figure mark, usually they will include some form of driver preparation service along with physical and mental training. Each company is set up differently so this is something you will have to discuss with them.

If you get a good management agency, life is a lot easier and many more doors of opportunity will be opened up for your driver due to their relationships within the sport.

2 - Solo manager

When talking about a manager like this, I want you to think of someone like Tom Cruise's character Jerry Maguire.

This is a person who manages drivers (and maybe even athletes in different sports) on a smaller scale. They may work on their own or have very few staff working for them.

If they have the skills to manage, they know the industry well and they have enough contacts in the right place, these managers can be just as good – if not better – than some of the bigger agencies.

When working with a solo manager, as the parent you may be required to take a more active role by assisting with peripheral tasks. You will also play a big part in the decisions made, but many drivers have succeeded with this set up. You just need to make sure you get a good manager: someone who knows the industry, who is good at promoting your driver, who can sell and be creative.

It's usually better if a manager like this has worked within the industry with previous success – because you do not want them to be learning as they go and making costly mistakes at your expense. They need to have good relationships in the sport too, so people with influence at the higher levels will pick up the phone to them.

It's hard to say what a solo manager would charge because it varies depending on their track record and the value they provide, but expect to pay between £20,000 to £50,000 per year.

3 - Performance companies

Whereas the management agencies prioritise the career and commercial duties for drivers, with the performance aspects being outsourced, performance companies do the exact opposite.

Performance companies may claim to offer management or career advice but it isn't really their true area of expertise. So they usually lack the motorsport business/contractual law knowledge required to advance and protect a driver's career.

Race teams will not normally deal with performance companies in the same way they deal with management agencies or solo managers. When a good manager approaches a team, the team knows they need to be on their game.

Performance companies are valuable, but when it comes to management they take the 'Jack of all trades' approach. Their website offers driver coaching, physical training, mental coaching, nutritional evaluation, media training... and then, near the bottom of their services, they slip in career management and sponsorship assistance.

Often these companies are set up by ex-race drivers who are good at coaching but then decide they want to offer management services – even if they do not have the track record or necessary business skills to be effective in that area.

Don't get me wrong: there are some good managers who used to race, and I can name a few. But do your research on a manager if this is the case. Make sure they have already succeeded with drivers and ask their past/current clients for their opinions.

Be especially cautious if a manager approaches you when they are still regularly racing themselves, because managing a driver's career is a full-time job. If done correctly, your manager shouldn't even have the time to go racing themselves, so you most likely won't be their biggest priority.

You need a manager to virtually bleed for your driver and their career, not just to have you there as an extra income stream.

Performance companies are great if you hire them to concentrate on what they are really good at (helping your driver perform better) but be cautious if they propose to look after the career of your child. Make sure they can really hold their own and be taken seriously when sat across the table from an F1 team boss or a potential big corporate sponsor.

You obviously get what you pay for in this world, so prices can range a lot here. But expect to pay between £15,000 and £60,000 per year for a performance company.

4 - The genuine helper

Now this last category is not something I would normally advise people to do. But having said that, I have seen it work extremely well in the past, so never say never...

The genuine helper is an individual who fulfils a lot of the roles that a manager would, but they are doing it for very little pay (or free of charge) because they want to be a part of your driver's journey and they genuinely want to assist.

This could be a family member, a friend you have in motorsport or someone else who you trust.

Once again, the effectiveness of this route comes down to the ability of the individual – because they may struggle to be any benefit to you if they do not know the industry very well or they lack the business acumen required. They must really come across well in order to pull this off.

To give you a good example of this working very well, let me tell you a quick (true) story...

The story of a school janitor

There was once a school janitor in New Zealand called Grant. Grant not only proved how this fourth category can work but he also proved just how much impact a single person can have on a driver's career.

Grant loved motorsport and he had been involved in it for a long time. He was mainly known for his journalism skills where he contributed to many different motorsport publications and he ran his own motorsport magazine called *SpeedSport*.

On top of this, he was an influential force behind the SpeedSport Scholarship in New Zealand – which was a driver shootout designed to help drivers step up from karting to cars. Each year the winner of the scholarship would be handed a free season's worth of racing.

This is something we don't see enough of in modern motorsport by the way. I really want to create a scholarship like this one day.

Anyway, drivers Shane Van Gisbergen, Richie Stanaway, Nick Cassidy and Liam Lawson, to name a few, are some of those who won the scholarship and went on to become professional race drivers.

When Liam Lawson won that scholarship in 2015, Grant saw a lot of potential in Liam. He took it upon himself to help raise the finance that Liam would need to chase his F1 dream.

Grant did whatever he could to open up doors of opportunities for Liam. This even saw the two of them fly to America (they had to raise sponsorship even to pay for their airfare...) to compete in another scholarship that gifted the winner $200,000 towards their racing on the Mazda Road To Indy programme. This meant the winner would effectively get a full season of USF2000 paid for.

Unfortunately, Liam didn't manage to win that scholarship. So Grant being Grant, he went back to the drawing board and continued to work on his sponsorship strategy.

Grant's main mission was to raise enough money through sponsorship and investments to give Liam the chance to race in Europe. In 2018, he managed it.

Whether you were a company owner of a small, medium or large business in New Zealand, you were most likely going to get a call from Grant. He contacted everyone he could in order to talk to them about his young protégé who was "going to make it to F1".

Grant's hard work paid off. Using a combination of sponsorship and driver investment, Grant had accumulated enough financial backing for Liam to compete in the 2018 ADAC Formula 4 championship, plus all Liam's living/travel expenses during his time in Europe.

Liam went on to finish second in the F4 championship and he followed this up by winning the Toyota Racing Series back in New Zealand. Liam's results and driving style then attracted the attention of the Red Bull Junior programme and they signed him soon after.

This may sound impressive, which it does, but it's only half the story because Grant not only did most of the fundraising on his own, but he did it while he was holding down his regular job as a school janitor.

Grant was making ends meet whilst juggling his nightshift and dedicating every other waking minute to raising funds, writing Liam's newsletters, organising interviews with the media and liaising with Liam's current sponsors.

As you will know, just getting the finances to race in F4 and attracting backing from an F1 team is tough enough. But for Grant it was only the beginning. When Liam stepped up a category and the cost of competing doubled each year, it was again up to Grant to source most of the funding to make this happen.

Grant worked tirelessly in these early days... and to this day he still is.

If you have ever looked for sponsorship for racing, I think you will appreciate just how hard it is to get companies interested in joining you.

On top of all this, Grant would partially fulfil the management role: where he would deal with race teams and carry out the day-to-day running of Liam's career.

I have never heard of anyone going to these lengths for a driver. That's why I will always regard Grant as being one of the most outstanding people I have ever worked with in motorsport.

Every driver would give their right arm (if they didn't need it for driving) to have someone like Grant by their side.

If you find a trustworthy person who has the skills of a manager and can genuinely help, I advise you to welcome them with open arms if you don't already have a manager in place. These people can be pure gold.

Just make sure they know what they are talking about. They must be intelligent and racing savvy. They also need to uphold a good reputation and have good people skills so race teams will take them seriously.

If they have these qualities, they can be a good addition to your 'team'.

Seven things to look for

No matter which category of manager you choose to work with, there are things that they all must possess – and provide you with – if they are worth your hard-earned money.

They must...

1. Be trustworthy

   It goes without saying that the person you appoint to steer your child's career, must be someone of integrity and who can be trusted. I will admit it is very rare to find managers who are completely transparent and honest with you... but they are out there.

   OK, let's be realistic here: because when you hire a manager, you are the client and they are the service provider. If you work for clients and customers, you will know full well you don't tell your clients and customers everything. There are certain things they don't need to know. So having 100 percent transparency may not be realistic. But you do at least want someone who will not be using you for your money to help another driver on their books, and someone who is not making 'backhand commissions' from the budgets you pay the team.

   When you and your child are attempting to create a racing career, you are metaphorically going to war together. Your manager needs to be that person you can trust to be by your side, and the one who will help you advance.

The world of motorsport is a cut-throat place where everybody seems to be trying to take from you. Your manager can't be one of those people.

2. Have a good reputation

   Your manager should have a good track record, not only from what they have previously achieved but also by what their current and former clients say about them.

   There are no Google reviews for managers, so you are going to have to do your own research. You can ask around the paddock and speak with people or teams to get a good idea about someone. It really is a small world so there will always be someone who will know of the manager you are considering.

   There will always be disgruntled previous clients out there because sometimes parents do not like hearing certain truths, such as if said manager told them their child simply doesn't have the skill to become a professional driver, or couldn't sell them to teams due to their poor race results. But if you ask around you will get a good idea of how they performed and if they are worth hiring.

3. Be good problem solvers

   You will face some very complicated and difficult situations over the years, from awkward conversations with your race team to handling lawsuits to overcoming bad press. Your manager or agency needs to have the kind of problem-solving skills that will help seek resolution in those times. Believe me, they will happen.

   This is something you only really learn once your manager is tested but if you really feel they are not made of the mettle required to survive in such a tough sport, jump. Have something in your contract that gives you a get-out clause if you are not happy with their service.

4. Have a good work ethic

   Your manager or agency needs to work tirelessly for you. They need to be the ones who are still working into the night and actively achieving the targets you mutually agreed on.

   Work ethic is something a person cannot really fake. If they are not taking your calls, or not completing tasks they have been set by you or themselves, if they are procrastinating and not making the calls they should be, you will see this a mile off.

   Make sure they are self-driven and they are putting in the work you are paying them for.

5. Be connected

   It is an old viewpoint from the world of show-business but you could always tell how good an agent was by the size of their rolodex or address book. They need to know everyone who is anyone in the industry and be able to pick up the phone to them.

   You want to look for the same capability when it comes to your manager. I say this because if top teams, driver academies and manufacturer heads won't return the calls from your manager, this is not a good thing.

   You will have to gauge how connected your manager is as you go, but this is yet another important capability that is a must.

6. Be good at negotiating

   It is a manager's job to get you some good options for race seats, to know the market, to know what drives are available and to be able to negotiate with teams. They need to get you deals that you wouldn't get if you went it alone.

If so, they pay for themselves by the money they save you. If they charge you a management fee of $40k per year but they haggle with a team to get you a drive for $40k less than what you would have got it for if you contacted the team yourself, they have become a very good investment. You are then pretty much getting their management services for free that year.

They also need to have the power to demand certain aspects in the team contract. Maybe they can secure you the previous year's champion's car and engineer, or they can get you some extra testing. Either way they not only need to get the price down, but they must position you in the team with a preferential package.

This is something that all good managers have a history of doing.

7. Not be overstretched

   If you are considering a certain manager or management company, make sure that they haven't taken on too many drivers already, especially if they their current drivers have the same goals and are at the same career stage as you.

   The last thing you want is your manager being conflicted and maybe offering their other drivers the opportunities that you need for your career.

   In saying this, if the management company is big enough, and they have enough staff (account managers, coaches, etc) to give you the one-to-one attention that you require, then they still may prove to be very valuable to you.

   This is just something to keep in mind when talking to the various managers out there. Always ask yourself "Can they prioritise me or are they spread too thin?".

Face the truth

It is often said that a manager or a coach is only as good as their driver/s, and it's true.

You could have the best manager in the world, but if the driver is honestly not good enough to deserve a professional career or contract, they will still fail.

You as the parent and your child as the driver need to be very self-aware.

It is easy for us to believe we are better than we actually are. We can get deluded by our passion for the sport and our viewpoint can mislead us.

We have all done this by the way, myself included. When I was 17 I was convinced I would become an F1 driver – even though I had never even done a single car race at that point, I had no money to race and didn't even know where to start. With all these facts, I was still adamant that I would make it. Looking back now I realise I had no chance... but in my mind back then, it was fully possible.

It makes me laugh (even cringe) when I think of it now.

Back then I would have blamed my manager for not finding the opportunities, when in reality it was because I was not worthy of an opportunity because I had nothing. Nobody was going to offer me anything. Luckily my work ethic got me to a pretty good level in racing before I found my true passion of coaching, but F1 was never on.

This just goes to show how our perspective can cause delusion, so I want to warn you about this.

Always be truthful about your driver's level and their value in the sport. Benchmark them and be fully aware of their skill level and overall brand. This is what your manager has to work with. So expectations need to be aligned with whatever is truly possible, not with what you simply dream might happen.

Do managers look for sponsorship?

Most managers and management companies do not actively go out and raise sponsorship for you. They may offer sponsorship services like sponsorship activation, sponsorship contract negotiations, creating brochures or offering sponsorship advice. But you won't often find them knocking on the doors of CEOs, selling the sponsorship opportunities for you.

This is because it is so damned hard to find sponsorship – and many management companies are set up by ex-racing drivers so their ability to sell within the business world is not exactly one of their strengths. Even if they are not ex-racers, or if they would be pretty good at gathering sponsorship, they have too much on their plate already even to have the time to seek sponsorship.

It's easier to find sponsorship for drivers who are already high profile but very difficult for drivers who are in the early stages. Thinking back to Grant, who helped Liam Lawson, there must be more people like him out there – but it's up to you to find someone like that.

As you may well have found out already, seeking sponsorship is a relentless task that requires as much commitment as a full time job. It is a very hard sell for companies because the actual value a race driver can provide a company with, doesn't match the cost of the budgets nowadays.

A company would much rather spend $50k on a social media assault (which has a measurable performance, can be instantly adjusted, paused or stopped with no contractual issues, and will most likely get them the results they want) than spend $50k for a sticker on the side of a race car with some race tickets.

Sponsorship offers companies a lot more than that, but that is the viewpoint of most firms out there when you utter the word 'sponsorship'.

To give you a speed course and typical plan of attack when it comes to securing sponsorship, you follow something like the following steps:

Step 1 - Get clear on what you can offer

First you must fully understand what opportunities your child, their racing, their championship and motorsport on the whole could possibly help companies reach their financial goals.

Step 2 – Research

Next you need to research companies that, from the outside, look like they could benefit from what you are offering and are a good fit.

Step 3 - Get in front of them

Then it's time to get meetings with the decision-makers of the companies you have shortlisted, so you can elicit what their goals are. Once you know what challenges they are trying to overcome or what they want to achieve the following year, you can come away and design a valuable sponsorship package that will assist them.

Step 4 - Design your package and sell it

Once you have put a package together that delivers a tremendous return on investment for that particular company, you meet them again to present what you can actually provide.

Step 5 - Make amendments and draw up a contract

If they are ready to move forward and they would like to become a sponsoring partner, you draw up a contract for them and discuss terms until everybody involved is happy to sign.

Obviously this is just a blueprint example and it may be a quicker or longer process than this, but you get the idea of how much work goes into sponsorship hunting.

You are basically extracting all the ways in which motorsport can help companies, understanding individual companies' needs and communicating this to them in a way that creates a sale.

Then you must obviously deliver on what is claimed in the sponsorship contract and ensure that the sponsoring company receives the ROI they expect.

On top of all this, you then need to do whatever you can to renegotiate a sponsorship deal for the following season and gather more sponsors as you go.

You can see how much time this will take a management company to do, especially if they were doing it for all their drivers.

There will be management companies that would offer you this service, but they would most likely want a sizeable retainer to pay for their time – as well as commission on whatever sponsorship they secure.

This is always a risk on your behalf, though, because if you are paying them approximately £60,000 per year as a retainer, you need to trust that they will actually deliver. That's a risk most parents are not prepared to take.

So this is the Catch 22. Management companies don't offer a sponsorship-seeking service because they do not have the time or expertise to do so, and parents won't pay for them even if they do because they don't want to risk wasting money.

What a predicament...

Become self-taught

If you are taking the sponsorship mission yourself, I have written a book that will help you called *Get The Drive*. No, that is not an advert by the way, I just want to let you know there is material already out there that will help you make sense of things.

Someone I know well who has an impressive sponsorship track record is Brian Sims. He also has a great motorsport sponsorship book available, so check his out as well.

So... do you need a manager?

Even though the chapter name is the same as this subheading, I have left it until now to answer the question, because I wanted to give you all the facts first.

If you have read this chapter fully, you will already be halfway to answering this question.

For me, a manager is needed in these situations:

1. When a driver is transitioning from karts to cars and they need someone who can hold their hand through the process, get them into a good team and put the required training in place
2. When a driver has achieved good results and is now ready to attract the attention of manufacturers or young driver programmes
3. When the driver's family feel overwhelmed, underprepared or like they are being taken advantage of by race teams and others in the sport. They may need someone to take the reins in order to avoid costly mistakes

Only you can decide when or if you need a manager to join your driver's team.

If I think back to my racing story, I got people to help me immediately because I didn't have a clue what I was doing. I somehow managed to get people to help and manage me for very little cost because I was willing to do most of the work, I had shown promise on track and I wouldn't take "No" for an answer.

You, however, may be more racing-savvy than I was, so you might not need assistance just yet.

Just remember a good manager can often get a race seat at a cheaper cost than parents or drivers can alone. This is because teams know they cannot pull the wool over the eyes of a good manager. Moreover, teams understand a manager can bring more drivers to them in the future so they want to look after them.

When a driver contacts a team directly, they see that driver as only being a one-off deal; a one-year transaction. So the team will turn up the volume on the budget to make sure they have a good pay day out of it.

Each team is different, but in essence a manager will get the cost down (if it's possible) and make sure you get offered a competitive package.

This again is dependent on what the driver has achieved beforehand, because a deal can't really be negotiated if the driver has finished outside the top 15 for the last two years. That's of no value to a team. The only value a driver in that position can bring is cash, so getting them to come down on their budget in this case will be challenging.

You probably don't need a manager if you are in this position. Instead you need a coach to help the driver perform better and earn the results that will help them negotiate the following year.

Summary

I hope this chapter has cast some light on the grey area of driver management.

It is a decision that only you can make because you know your situation, the goals you have and the level of your driver's skills. Put all this together and you can come up with your own conclusion.

Most managers will offer an annual contract but that will have a termination clause (with a notice period) included. So always remember you can try out management without too much obligation to see if it works for you.

Either way, ideally you want someone working with you who will go that extra mile for your driver, who is intelligent, connected, trustworthy and has a good reputation. If you partner with somebody like that and your driver delivers the required results, things will be looking good.

CHAPTER 17
RUNNING OUT OF MONEY

When you are writing a book that focuses on a race driver's career, how can we not touch upon the subject of money?

Something that I always have to remind myself and my clients is that motorsport is exactly that... It's Motor Sport.

Not only does this title imply a driver must have competitive machinery in order to win, but the name of our sport also alludes to the fact that it's expensive to compete with a vehicle.

Motorsport is, has always been and will always be one for the most expensive sports on the planet. It's a pastime that requires its competitors to pay to play – and nothing in racing is cheap.

Also, nothing is as frustrating for a driver as when they are held back due to their finances. This sport punishes drivers who are good enough to win at the pinnacle of our sport yet don't get the chance due to their lack of funds.

I know plenty of drivers who are quicker (and all-round better) than most of the drivers on the current F1 grid. But due to them not being able to afford to walk that path, we never get to see them fight for the world title.

It is painful to see, but it's just the way it is at the moment.

I feel your pain

It's not just drivers who are frustrated by the money aspect of racing; parents also carry the burden.

If you were the one who introduced your child to racing at a young age, you were most likely the one who had to pay for their racing in the early days. As prices continued to rise over the years (as they climbed the racing ladder) you may have found that things started to get out of control financially.

The driver will often still look at the parent to help them source the extra finance needed, but things are not as easy as that.

This can play with you mentally. The situation of not being able to help your child chase their dream can leave you feeling guilty, helpless, regretful and lost. That's a lot of pressure for all involved and it can strain relationships as well as careers.

It was different for me when I raced because I was racing against my father's wishes, so I had to go out and find the money myself. I was only on a pizza delivery boy's wage (£1.50 per pizza delivery) so I had to get very creative and good at producing opportunities for myself in the racing world.

That means I fully understand how tough it can be.

What are you going to do?

When in a tough situation like this, you must refrain from falling for the 'woe is me' victim mindset or panicking. Instead it is time to accept the sport has always been like this and come up with a plan for what you are going to do about this challenge.

You can't blame the game, because this sport has been around a lot longer than we have. So we have no right to come along so late to the party and complain about how things are. Well, we can... and we often do... but it doesn't achieve anything.

To avoid complaining about things that are not going to change, you must put yourself into a resourceful mindset and come up with a plan (or many plans) for how you are going to overcome the financial challenge you are presented with.

Luckily. that is exactly what my younger self did.

My previous battle plan

I don't want to spend too much time talking about myself, but on this occasion it may explain things and help you decide what to do yourself.

I started late in racing with very little backing so my situation was the following:

1. I had no money or connections in the sport
2. I had no idea if I was even good enough to race
3. I had no karting experience
4. All I had was a stupidly big goal (F1) and I was willing to put everything into it
5. I was way older than other drivers who wanted to go to F1, who also had more talent and more money than me

My battle plan was to take things one step at a time.

First of all I knew I had to find a championship that I could actually afford. No matter how uncool the championship was, I just had to get on track and start racing. I would have raced lawnmowers if that was all I could get into.

Thankfully I didn't have to start racing on grass; instead I found a cheap Formula Ford car for sale and did the unthinkable thing of getting a bank loan to help me buy it.

I then rallied around, gathering as much sponsorship from local companies as I could. Between their money, the bank loan, favours from people in the sport (lending me tools and a trailer) plus the money I got from working as many jobs as possible, I managed to make it through a full season.

It was only a secondary Formula Ford championship, but it was enough for me to improve my driving skills. I learned how to get sponsorship, made some contacts in the sport and it gave me some kind of springboard into the industry.

In the second year I won the same championship and went on to compete at a decent level nationally before finding my true calling as a performance coach.

Along the way I worked as a coach at race schools, a race team mechanic, a demonstration driver and anything else I could that kept me working within the industry so I could be in among it all.

This helped me meet many people within the industry and advanced my understanding of how things work in the sport. It was a wild ride where I learned a lot about racing – and myself.

Motorsport constantly kicked me when I was down, and it tortured me mentally. I found myself in some embarrassing situations but I believe I went through all that just so I could help other drivers (and now parents) who are facing similar challenges.

What's your battle plan?

As you can tell, my battle plan was to find a cheap championship and do all I could to raise the money needed to compete. It wasn't pretty and it wasn't easy but my approach may give you some ideas for what you can do.

In order for you to come up with your plan of attack, the first port of call is to get very clear on the exact situation your driver is in right now.

If you are struggling for the finance needed, we can allow your focus to become a little more short term focused. By all means take a quick peek at your driver's long term goals, but we need to quickly get their (and your) mind on what the plan is for the next 12 months.

If you cannot afford the career path or championships that you would ideally like your driver to compete in, you may need to pivot and think outside the box.

Essentially, all you need is to keep your driver on track, in something. Actually, get them in anything.

When you do not have the money to do what you want, you have to broaden your mind and ask yourself: "What can we do that will keep the driver active, no matter what that is?"

This is not an ideal position to be in, but if money has dried up then it's better to be competing in a championship that is beneath your driver's level, than have them sat at home doing nothing all year.

You need to keep them active, no matter what that is.

So take the time to come up with a backup plan that can keep them competing. That way you have something that will give you a 'vehicle' for attracting new sponsorship deals. Even racing at club level as you gather sponsors is better than nothing.

Think about this and always have a plan in mind.

Everyone loves a winner

At the end of the day if your driver is going to succeed in this sport, they absolutely must be winning at some level – especially if they haven't got access to a big budget. If they haven't got a big bank balance, they must possess a big 'winning balance'.

Quite simply they must stand out and make noise for the right reasons in the sport if they want to advance.

You can view a driver as you view a car. If you were to buy a car to race that didn't have the speed to win, that was unreliable and caused nothing but trouble, you would get rid of it as fast as possible.

That's how top race teams and manufacturers view drivers. If a driver hasn't got the speed, their results are inconsistent or their attitude isn't what they want, they will be disposed of immediately.

So again, your driver must be winning races and be known for consistently being fast.

This is why I say that if you cannot afford to compete at the front of a higher profile championship, then get your driver into a lower profile championship, but dominate it. Not only will they grab the headlines, which can open up career doors, but they will sharpen their skills and learn how to win. This is something that drivers do when they are struggling with finances.

Felix's story

If you look at someone like Felix Rosenqvist, he demonstrated how staying in a championship until you win it (due to not having enough money to step up a category) can be a good plan.

Felix spent a whopping six seasons racing at the Formula 3 level. At the time you could hear people muttering their criticisms about how he should either move on or stop racing, but he didn't listen. He continued to stay in that championship year after year until he won and created career advancing opportunities for himself.

Here is his Formula 3 record:

- 2010 - ATS F3 Series - P5
- 2011 - F3 Euro Series - P5
- 2012 - FIA European F3 - P3
- 2013 - FIA European F3 - P2
- 2014 - FIA European F3 - P8
- 2015 - FIA European F3 - P1

Looking at this, most drivers would have given up and maybe shifted to GTs following his P8 finish in the 2014 championship. Luckily for him he didn't quit; he gave it one more go after being offered an opportunity by Prema and Lance Stroll that he couldn't refuse, and this proved to be a good move.

Within two years of his last F3 season, he was a professional driver in Formula E. He then went on to become a full-time IndyCar driver.

Not bad!

I want you to think of this when deciding what your driver should be doing.

Be prepared to work in the dirt

I fully understand that F3 is a high level and you may not even have the finances to compete there. But you can do the equivalent in whatever level your driver can afford.

I would prefer your driver to slowly build their brand in the sport by dominating club level series as they gather many small sponsors, pester teams in the next level tiers and master their craft, rather than wishing to have the money to race in a higher category, only to fail to get the money together each year.

Your driver is better off racing in anything rather than nothing. Do not let them get too precious about what they race and demonstrate to them that they must earn their way up. If they truly love racing, they will put the work in and be patient. It's also a good way to test their commitment.

This is the same in the entrepreneurial world. Many super-successful entrepreneurs didn't jump straight into the company that they are currently known for. Instead they spent their early years selling at market stalls, hustling and working in the dirt.

If drivers do not come from a family that can easily pay for them to race, they must walk a similar path to these entrepreneurs. They must build their own future.

Outside the box hustling

Apart from switching championships (because you may be halfway through the season already) you may have to get creative when you lack the finance to compete.

Your driver will have to constantly pitch themselves to the teams they want to race for; they must be very active in looking for sponsors; they must do all the fundraising they can and create business deals with people who can assist – both inside and outside of racing.

If your child is too young to do these things, I'm afraid it will be down to you or someone else who could help out.

If your driver has achieved very impressive results in the past, contacting teams with the promise that they will win in their car is actually a good tactic. If you speak to enough teams, you could find one team that needs the results. Maybe they can subsidise the price of the drive or even offer you a few free races in order to get their car at the front of the grid.

If your driver is slightly older and has some good car race results, offering their driving services to gentleman drivers (Am drivers) in the GT categories, can be sellable. Your driver can coach and race alongside the gentleman driver – and together they can go and win the title. This is a tactic many drivers use when they are struggling for money. and it can work really well.

If money is super-tight then your son or daughter can work as a team driver coach for a year or so. This way they will be earning good money, they will be at the race events and most likely they will get the occasional run in the race cars for the team.

It's never easy when you have a lack of finances, so you just need to hustle and try absolutely everything you can. But, again, this work ethic has to come from the driver.

There is nothing worse when the mother or father are working their tail off to help their child race, but the child themselves doesn't lift a finger to help. Please do not let this happen. They need to prove their commitment and more than outwork their parents.

I always talk about having people that will bleed to help you in your career, but really the driver has to bleed more than anyone else.

Caravan to F1 winner

It is so easy for us to hit false limits and take on limiting beliefs when pursuing such a tough dream. We can come up with affirmations like "this sport is only for the super wealthy" or "It's impossible to succeed without having the cash." But there are drivers out there who made it to the highest levels of our sport, with next to no money.

A past client of mine, Esteban Ocon, was a driver who did this. When he was karting, he and his family were putting all their money into his racing. So much so that they all lived in a caravan in order to maximise the money they could spend on Esteban's racing.

They sold their house, put their jobs on hold and went all in. While they did this, he was impressing people on track. In doing so, he grabbed the attention of a driver programme called Gravity Sport Management (who I was working for at the time). As a result of his speed and commitment, we signed him up and paid for most of his junior car racing career.

Fast forward a few years, he got picked up by Toto Wolff and he was soon winning his first F1 race.

Other F1 drivers like Lewis Hamilton, Valtteri Bottas and Alexander Albon also lacked the personal finances to pay their way to F1. They all hustled... and at some point they caught the eye of people who could assist them financially.

Even though the list of drivers who have done this is short, it is still possible to create a racing career without having a lot of money in the bank. Again thinking of Liam Lawson, his family didn't have the money to pay for even F4, but he (and Grant) have managed to make a lot of noise in the sport.

If we look at championships other than F1, there are hundreds, if not thousands of drivers who have managed to create careers even though they lacked the finances. The sportscar route is littered with drivers who didn't have much personal money but still secured paid drives.

Yet they proved their worth via their results, their work ethic and their commitment to their dream. They also had personalities that attracted people to them. These are all things your driver must be good at if they are to succeed without having much money behind them.

Bills and dreams

Bills and dreams is a saying I came up with to describe what it takes to advance your racing career when you do not have enough money to race what you want.

The basic principle is that every person in this sport either wants to pay their bills or achieve their dreams.

This is good to know... because if you can focus on the certain individuals who can help pay for your driver's racing or offer them an opportunity, all you have to do is find out what they want most.

If they want to earn more money (pay their bills) you must figure out how you can provide that for them, directly or indirectly.

If you find someone who wants to achieve their dreams, you need to find out how you can help them do that.

For example, if a team is desperately seeking more finances, maybe you can find them a driver who does have a lot of money. Alternatively, you can lead them to a sponsorship or a business deal that will help them. In return, you can do a deal that will get you a subsidised drive.

Keeping teams in mind, if you find one that desperately needs good results because they have been beaten too often over recent years – and your driver has proven that they can win in any car – your driver can sell themselves to them on a performance-based deal.

This was when I got cocky on the phone to teams. I would find struggling teams and literally say: "Get me in your car and I will win for you" or "I will not sleep until I have put your car up the front."

Yes, I really was that cocky.

But it worked from time to time. It meant I had to deliver, but it got me into seats that I wouldn't have had if I did what most drivers did – and just called up to ask what their budget was.

The two main currencies needed for a driver to create a successful career are cash or speed. As a driver you need to help race teams and manufacturers achieve their dreams or pay their bills.

This also goes for anyone else who could assist your driver. Maybe you could help a PR company by getting them to work with a top team, and in return you get commission or the PR company helps your driver with their services. This kind of thinking can get you far.

Always remember bills and dreams. Help people get what they want, and you get what you want.

Summary

I have purposely bombarded you in this chapter because once again, this subject is so individual to your and your driver's situation. So hopefully there will be something in here that inspires your own thoughts or I have planted some seeds in your mind that will give you an epiphany in a few days.

Either way, if you do not have the money, you need to work like hell and get creative.

Add value to others, be seen and keep thinking of new approaches.

CHAPTER 18
WHEN YOUR RACE TEAM ARE NOT PERFORMING

We have a long list of things that are difficult to deal with in motorsport – and having a race team that is consistently underperforming is near the top of that list.

There you are, pouring your hard-earned money into your team's pocket... yet weekend after weekend they continue to let you down and not deliver the service you expected. In this situation you are left feeling trapped and powerless as you watch them destroy your driver's championship campaign.

I am sure you have already been through this experience – because most drivers and parents have. It is a constant battle but when it does happen, I urge you to do whatever you can to handle things correctly so you can salvage the situation without harming your driver's reputation in the sport.

The best way for me to offer advice on this topic is to run you through the whole process from beginning to end, from team selection to handling the teams when things are not going to plan.

All the advice I give here is tried and tested – and the kind of protocols top management companies have in place as they handle race teams.

Team selection

The obvious first port of call is to take things back to before the relationship even starts with a team, by ensuring that you do all you can to select the right team for your driver.

I will keep this part brief because we have already covered this subject in the earlier chapter. But just remember it's not always as obvious as you think when it comes to team selection.

Yes, they need to have a proven track record and they must have shown they can do a good job on track the previous year. But you must also make sure they are a good fit for you and your driver.

They must tick as many of the following boxes as possible:

1. They are fairly priced and offer you what you need
2. They provide competitive machinery
3. They help prepare the driver
4. They employ accomplished members of staff
5. They look and act professionally
6. They are sponsor-friendly, and accommodating to your sponsors' needs
7. They are trustworthy
8. They create a good working atmosphere
9. They are hungry to win

There are other aspects that may be taken into consideration, like teams that have good contacts with F1 junior programmes or teams that can help advance your driver's career in some way. But essentially, we need to look at teams as companies and ensure the service they provide will, at least on paper, give you a shot at having a successful time with them.

These are all standard things to look for. Some may be more relevant to you than others and some you will have to ask around to find out, but these points can help you come to a good decision.

Common challenges

Once you are all signed up and racing gets under way, you begin to see what your team is really all about. This is when the relationship kicks onto the next level... when you are either happy as Larry or pulling your hair out.

If you are pulling your hair out, remind yourself you are not alone here. Plenty of drivers on your grid will be going through a similar situation. Common challenges drivers face are when...

- The team and driver do not agree on the reason for the lack of pace (the driver is convinced their driving is OK so they are blaming the car, whereas the team are blaming the driver)
- The relationship with the engineer isn't working
- The teammate has a quicker engine or better equipment/treatment
- They are having too many reliability problems
- The team are making too many avoidable mistakes
- The team are not organised enough
- The team have started overcharging for things, or not fulfilling what is in the contract
- The team do not seem motivated or committed enough; they have a part-time approach
- The team have taken on too much and spread themselves too thin

- The driver doesn't like the way the team boss or team manager treats them

These are just to name a few things that constantly pop up in the average race season.

The business model

As I mentioned before, most race teams are created on a business model that requires them not only to get good results but also to keep the money coming in. This leads them to structure their company in a way that allows them to do this. And, depending on how their previous season went and how they are doing financially, they can be forced to make decisions that serve themselves first – before you and your driver.

From your perspective as the customer, when you have paid good money and you are expecting a top service in return, you can easily get upset when they don't fulfil their side of the bargain – and rightly so by the way. You are totally correct to see things this way.

However, when the team is busting their backside to balance the needs of all their drivers as well as meeting the needs of their staff and their bottom line, they sometimes take actions and have certain viewpoints that are not aligned with what you want.

So it is inevitable that you will run into some disputes with teams, just because of the nature of how things are set up. So my first piece of advice would be to accept and expect that.

Fully accept that these moments will pop up from time to time. So instead of this reality bringing you and your driver down, plan for when something does happen and for how you can best resolve it.

When things go down

If you are in the pre-season or pre-contract phase, you obviously put out as many of these potential fires (situations) as you can. That means you get off on the right foot and cover future problems you may encounter.

Once you're in the season though, when issues occur and you are unhappy with the way things are, it is all about how you handle it and communicate things with the team.

If you just scream, shout and complain about things, the team will often react with resentment. And it won't be long until the relationship breaks down and you are both suing each other. If things go that far, it won't help your driver's reputation in the paddock. So this should be avoided... unless they really deserve it.

What I have seen work best is when you, your driver, plus the manager or coach (if you have them) all take it upon yourselves to create the kind of environment within the team where everyone is pulling together.

This means that no matter who is dropping the ball, whether it is your driver or it is the team, you all come together to tackle these issues as a unit.

In practical terms, that means that following each main test event and race weekend, you all jump on a zoom call or meet in person to discuss how the event went.

Together you can cover what was good and not so good about your driver's performance and the team's performance, discussing the lessons from the event. This will help everyone progress and you can all form mutual goals for next time.

If you have this in place, and everyone understands you are all there to help each other win, this can put out many of the fires that come up during a season.

Remember: you will have times when you become annoyed by your team. But, like any relationship, if the communication is good and you all leave your egos at the door, you can be very honest with each other and turn each issue into an opportunity to move forward.

I have seen this work really well because it aligns everyone's perspective and prevents the 'Them and Us' situation. It also prevents outbursts from either party due to bottling up their true feelings and thoughts over time.

It's never too late to create this growth environment approach, to show you are there to learn and assist the progress as a collective. In doing this, nobody in the team will feel threatened or judged, and you will take on the philosophy of: Together Everyone Achieves More.

Fulfil all duties

Something I have seen destroy team/driver relationships is if your driver fails to uphold their half of the deal. They may start missing team simulator or prep days, they may be slow responding to emails/messages or the big one – which you may be responsible for – when team bills are paid late.

All these things (especially the last one) wind a team up and stress the relationship. Once it happens, they may start to treat you differently to the other drivers in the team – and things can begin to fall apart from there.

So make sure your driver more than fulfils their half of the deal, and wins the team over due to their work ethic and by fulfilling obligations. Half that battle is won if the team actually likes your driver – and as a result they genuinely want your driver to win.

It may be called motorsport but it is still a people sport. If your driver can win people over, their time with a race team (and in their career) will go much smoother.

If you find you keep having similar problems with different teams, then ask yourself: what could the driver be doing that isn't helping them win the team over? Is it their attitude, their driving, their approach, their professionalism... or are the team being made to wait for their money?

There just might be something there.

I'm not blaming you or your driver here; I just like to look inward first, before blaming the teams.

If you think this might be applicable to your situation, have a straightforward chat with the team manager or boss to get to the root problem. Then have an even more direct discussion with your driver to get them to shape up... just in case the driver's camp is doing something by accident that is causing friction.

Get things in writing

If – after being careful with your initial team selection, having created a healthy relationship with the team, having regular performance reviews and your driver is fulfilling their duties – the team are still misbehaving and not fulfilling their duties, it's time to get firm with them.

Start off by getting things in writing via email following the race weekend, explaining your concerns and what you would like to resolve. This email will act as your legal proof that you communicated your concerns and that you were actively seeking ways to address the situation. Always have things like this in wiring to get things clear, and just in case matters go further.

A team is there to serve you; you are paying them. So you have the full right to demand that change happens – and happens quickly if needed. Obviously remain amicable in your discussions with them, but clearly communicate what you want as a customer.

Once you have communicated via writing, ideally you will have a face-to-face meeting with the team manager or team owner to address things.

Manage expectations

Other disputes that drivers and teams have are when the driver joins a team that has been down the bottom of the grid for many years... yet they still join up thinking they can win, or be consistently in the top ten positions.

This is where the expectations of the driver do not meet reality. So before your driver joins a team that hasn't achieved any real success up to that point, your driver must fully come to terms with the fact that the team may not be capable of giving them a competitive package just yet.

It's great if they do, and your driver takes them to the front. But things don't often happen that way.

This means your driver has to manage their own expectations – and go into a team ready to work harder than other drivers. They may need to go that extra mile to help the team improve.

This is when your driver needs to make sure they approach things with an open mind and create the growth environment I mentioned earlier.

Your driver will have to be patient; they will have to run the show and make it their mission to get themselves and their team further up the grid.

If approached in the correct way, racing for a small and unproven team can be very character-building for a driver. This may be something to remember at some point in your driver's career.

Summary

Race teams are there to win, but they also have to make money to survive. For them it is a constant chicken-and-egg situation where they need to pivot and adapt in order to stay alive in this sport.

This means they have different priorities to drivers, so keep that in mind when challenges arise.

The word 'team' is important here. That team environment needs to be created so everyone can openly express themselves and grow together. Race teams are not very good at doing this, so it may be down to your driver to bring this to the party.

In summary, be selective when choosing a team. Do your research, make sure everything is clear legally to begin with, create the environment needed, have regular performance review meetings and hit things head on if there is still a problem.

Adapt this to your approach and it should help you have a smoother experience.

CHAPTER 19
DOES MY KID HAVE WHAT IT TAKES?

Virtually every parent gets to the point when they start asking the ultimate question: "Does my kid have what it takes?"

Some parents fear the answer, because they don't want to see their beloved child disappointed or for them to feel they are not good enough, or they have failed. Other parents fear it because they themselves get a kick out of their child's racing, so they don't want things to change or end.

Some parents just want to find out the truth. They may want to know whether their child has the potential to create a career as a driver before they sink even more money into the money pit of motorsport. Or they may want their child to stop racing and get a proper job.

Either way, gaining clarity and seeking the truth is something most of us have to face in any career, so we can plan things going forward.

In this chapter we will discuss ways to find out whether your driver does actually have the necessary skills to make a career in this sport so you can progress on the best path for them.

It all starts with the goal

When you are assessing a person's ability in any sport or industry, the first step is to understand what they are trying to achieve long term.

If you know someone's main goal, you can easily assess whether their current skill levels, individual attributes and approach all come together to provide them with the potential for reaching it.

In the business world, if a person claimed they wanted to be the next Steve Jobs or Elon Musk, and you could see they possessed attributes, grand visions and personal skills that were similar to Steve and Elon, you would naturally think they had a shot.

However, if this person had certain self-sabotaging characteristics or skills that were well below par – and they didn't possess the kind of work ethic or discipline to improve those areas – you wouldn't give them very good odds.

It's essentially the same for drivers. In fact, it's even easier for us to give a verdict on a driver's potential because we have a lot more data points to draw conclusions from compared to the entrepreneurial world.

Due to data analysis, video footage, teammate comparison, results on track and their conduct off track, we can normally tell quite quickly if a driver has what it takes to succeed in this sport.

In saying all this, you still need to first understand what the driver's main goal is.

So if you are at the point of asking this main question, sit your driver down and get fully clear on what their aspirations are.

It must be *their* goal

This can be quite a sensitive subject because very often the parents of drivers have their own goals for their children, whereas the children themselves don't really care as much. This is when you get the interesting situation where the parent is working their tail off to help their child, but the child isn't putting in the necessary effort.

This is a recipe for disaster and it won't end well.

If so, you will have some frustrating times ahead – and over time your relationship with your child will become strained. What's more, you run the risk of ignoring the truth about their potential.

If you are reading this book, I don't think you will be one of those parents. But if you do find yourself getting carried away from time to time and you seem to desire the racing dream more than your child, just pause for a moment. Remember this is all about them and what they want.

If a driver doesn't possess the passion to race at their very core, they will simply not commit fully and they will never succeed. The sport is too difficult to approach in a half-assed fashion.

One of the main attributes a person needs to succeed is their passion and desire to do so. If that is missing, they lack the fuel required to reach their goals. So your driver has to be seriously hungry to reach their goal.

That's step number one

What I just mentioned there is the first port of call when you are trying to understand whether your driver has what it takes. They need to possess the hunger.

Actually, they need to be starving for racing... and have it as their number one love in life.

If you find you are the one who does most of the work, or that you have to nag at your driver to put the work in, I'm afraid your driver may just be missing the number one essential ingredient to make a career in this sport.

Nobody gets anywhere in this sport without bleeding for it.

As a driver you can have all the speed and talent in the world, but if your heart isn't really in it and you do not put all your effort into it, you are very unlikely to become a professional race driver.

Remember that when works teams or manufacturers choose drivers to drive for them, they use the same assessment process as any other company does when looking to employ somebody. A normal company will interview a prospective employee, look at their CV, try to judge their potential, and aim to understand their personality to see if they are a good fit. The company will only offer somebody the job if they feel this person can fulfil the position and help the company progress.

This is exactly the same for professional race teams who can offer your driver a paid position.

They need to see determination, a strong work ethic, the right kind of attitude and speed on track. These are all difficult things to possess as a driver if they are not fully committed to their craft and they do not have passion for the sport.

The required attributes

Given you are reading this chapter and wondering if your driver has what it takes, I am going to presume your driver's goal is a big one. I will also presume they are dreaming of becoming a professional driver – and they want to earn their living from being a race driver.

If so, and you want to know if they have what it takes, it's time to run you through a list of attributes drivers should have if they are to succeed.

Let's look at the main qualities drivers must have if they are to make it all the way to the elite levels of the sport. These are applicable whether they are aiming for F1, IndyCar, NASCAR, Le Mans or any other professional championship at the top of our sport. They must have the following attributes:

1. Outright speed on track
2. Strong performance in all weather conditions
3. Impressive race craft
4. Ability to drive at a high standard consistently
5. Good decision making
6. A good understanding of car dynamics and engineering
7. Very good car control
8. Ability to adapt to change of grip and imbalance in the car
9. Understanding of how to drive in whatever way the current car requires
10. Ability to learn very quickly
11. Mental strength and the ability to handle pressure/adversity well
12. High levels of self-confidence and self-belief
13. Very good leadership skills
14. A promotable personality
15. Hard work on their craft

This list of 15 attributes may look long but I promise there are many things missing here. Still, these are the kinds of things professional teams will look for in a driver. Plus, they are the kind of qualities a driver simply must have if they are to make a career in racing.

This list also hits home just how much commitment and training a driver needs if they are going to take their racing seriously. It is a full-time job for them and it takes time.

Score your driver

You do not need to be daunted as you look at this list; it is just an idea of what professional teams look for in drivers. It should give you clarity so you can assess where your driver is at.

Next, I want you to score your driver (out of 10) on each item mentioned in that list.

So if you take the first item (outright speed on track) give them a rating that sums up their current speed. if you think they are normally about half a second off the pace of their teammates, you may score them a 6/10,because they are barely above average in that area.

Go through the whole list and see what scores you come up with. You can even work out what their percentage is, giving you a very good idea of their level.

I do this with every driver I work with at the beginning of our coaching relationship. We get clear on their goal and subjectively we assess where they are now.

This gives me clarity for where they are at and what work needs to be done. There Is no reason why you can't do this with your own driver.

In simple terms

To give you this again in simple terms, the basic process that will help you understand your driver's current level is to get clear on the following:

Their main goal → The required attributes → Their scores in each area

Once you have completed this process and you are being very honest with your scores, you can reveal the truth. You can either make decisions from there or put training in place that will help them improve the areas where they are under par.

Who to ask

If you want to ensure your scores are accurate, by all means ask somebody else (who is in the know) to assess your driver.

This is the equivalent of getting a second opinion from your doctor. You may have a sense of your driver's skill levels in all the aforementioned areas, but it is always good to get the honest opinion of someone who has been in the industry for a while, and who knows what they are doing.

If you do this, make sure you ask a person who has worked with many drivers who have gone on to create successful careers, so they know what to look for. It also has to be someone who has no axe to grind or financial benefit to gain from giving you their opinion.

For example, if you showed your list to a race team that desperately wanted to sign your driver up next year, and you asked them to score your driver in some of the areas you have highlighted (or at least give their feedback), they may say something like: "Ah yes, your kid is 8 to 10 in each area. They have massive potential!"

They might just be saying that because they want to sign your driver up. So keep this in mind when selecting the people to ask.

At this point, you know what your driver is eager to achieve. You know what attributes are required in order to achieve that goal. Now all you need to do is find someone who can give you an honest snapshot of your driver and give things to you straight.

Clarity and honesty is power when you are pursuing a goal, and this simple process is the most straightforward and direct way for finding out the truth.

How long to give them

Your driver will obviously not be scoring high enough in some of the areas you highlight, so we need to give your driver time to improve these areas before calling it a day.

So once you have all your scores and you have exposed the areas that need improvement, it is time to design their very own self development plan to help them do that.

If they need to improve their results, find out what it is about their driving or mental performance that needs work. Then get the right person, training or system in place to help them do that.

Off-track skills must never be ignored. If, for example, you notice your driver's people skills or their personal brand are not what they need to be, double down on these areas.

Remember this is a sport run by people. People hold the key to your driver's career because they are the ones who can offer opportunities. So your driver needs to be able win people over and inspire others. That means they must possess people, sales and leadership skills.

With all this in mind, we have to have some kind of timeframe in mind – because their goal may be age sensitive and you only have so much money to keep this dream going. So it's important that you put a timeframe on this.

Your driver's current position (or main goal) will determine how much time they have to improve. But to speed things up they can create smaller personal performance goals – and put dates on them.

To give you an idea of what they may look like, you can have goals and timeframes in place like this:

- To master the braking technique for this car within the next two race weekends
- To attract two more sponsors in the next two months
- To book a place on a sales course in the next week
- To book a place on a leadership course in the next week
- To have a mental assessment done in the next month

I prefer to have goals related to their actual personal performance/skills instead of just something like: "To win a race in the next four race meetings." Results-based goals are OK but they must always be reverse-engineered so the driver understands what to actually do.

Their mind needs to be focused on what needs to be done, not just what they want overall.

We need to help the driver possess the skills that automatically deliver those race wins. You need to build a driver so they gain the results they deserve, rather than just shooting for a certain result.

Each driver has their own rate of progression, natural abilities and goals, so I could never tell you how long to give your driver. But if you follow what I have said in this chapter and you begin to see progress (on track and within your self-created list) from there you can be the judge for how long you give your driver to achieve their goal.

An ultimatum

If you are paying for your driver to race and you need your driver to apply themselves more, you can always offer an ultimatum.

You could give them one more season to prove they have what it takes and to give it everything they have, otherwise they have to fund themselves.

Some people will see this as pressure, but for me it's the 'Welcome to life kid' kind of approach.

One thing I won't stand for is a driver who is spending their parent's money on their racing, yet not giving things their full effort. That hurts me and echoes traits of a spoiled child.

If your driver is doing this, there has to be a time when you provide some tough love and wake them up with a time-sensitive goal.

We have to prepare our children for how tough life is. This is a way to help them step up – or at least find out if they truly love their sport or not.

CHAPTER 20
HOW TO GET SPOTTED AND PICKED UP

The previous chapter "Does my kid have what it takes?" leads us straight into the topic of helping your driver getting spotted by somebody who can offer them an opportunity in racing.

Every single race driver who has managed to achieve a professional career in motorsport had a certain turning point when somebody offered them something that turned out to be a complete game-changer for them.

For some, it was when a Formula 1 young driver programme offered them a contract, or when a manufacturer contacted them to offer them a GT drive or when a big sponsor noticed them and offered them sponsorship.

Game-changing moments come in many guises. They can be big opportunities like an approach from a Formula 1 academy, or smaller opportunities like when a top team offers your driver a position.

Whatever it is, your driver will not be able to advance very far if they are not given a shot by somebody who has the power to offer them a leg-up in their career.

This will take some work, but if you help your driver possess the very attributes I covered in the previous chapter and make sure you both have a plan in place, your driver will stand a much better chance of being spotted.

What scouts look for

I like talking about this topic because I have worked as a scout for Formula 1 driver programmes and management companies. So I can share exactly what I look for when I'm hunting for the next driver to sign up.

Over the years I scouted and helped drivers including Esteban Ocon, Romain Grosjean, Liam Lawson and Oliver Bearman, to name a few. These drivers were picked up because they all had the qualities that the big hitters in our sport wanted. So all I have to do here is share with you what these drivers had that helped them attract attention.

To make it easy to understand, these are the three main areas scouts look for:

1. A driver's actual driving skills. They must be fast and have good results
2. A driver's attitude and reputation in the sport
3. If a driver has any kind of political advantage

The first area (driving skill and results) is a pretty obvious starting point. If a scout sees a certain driver is always up the front and winning races, this puts that driver on their radar immediately.

Never forget a professional team or manufacturer needs a driver who is seriously fast. That's a race driver's top value. Speed is a driver's main currency.

Investors, programme managers and manufacturers haven't got the time to fully understand your driver's position and challenges. So they don't care if your driver has just had bad luck all year, if they are with a poor team or they haven't had the amount of testing that everyone else on the grid has. Instead they deal with black and white facts.

They just see the results and take things at face value.

Once your driver has achieved good results, scouts and programme managers will look further into that driver by assessing what their attitude and reputation is like.

They will want to know what the driver is like, whether or not they are a hard worker, if they have a good approach and if they are the kind of person who actually deserves a shot.

If a driver is quick but is a little shit to deal with – i.e. they are lazy or they have a bad attitude – most teams or manufacturers will avoid them... because that driver can easily act in a way that destroys their brand.

When I looked at a driver who obviously had the speed and ability to become a professional driver, I would ask around the paddock and talk to their team to understand more about them as a person. I would want to find out if that driver would embarrass me if I was to offer them an opportunity – and if they are somebody who deserves to succeed.

I will say this a thousand times: people run this sport.

If a driver is obnoxious or they will cause you headaches by the way they act, you won't want to help them out. Your driver must understand they need to win people over if they want to win long term.

Once a scout understands a driver is fast and they have a good attitude, it won't be long until they approach that driver...

Get them inspired

If a driver really wants to stand out, they must inspire others. This means by the way they drive and by the way they act when away from the track.

If a person of influence sees a driver out-driving their competitors in the wet, or overtaking their way to an impressive race win – and that same driver follows things up with a coherent and inspirational interview after the race – this is the kind of driver manufacturers will be falling over themselves to sign up.

Josef Newgarden is a good example of a driver that has this down.

I remember listening to him on stage at the 2022 Autosport Awards – and all the people in that room were gobsmacked at how well he communicated and held himself on stage. We are not used to race drivers being such good public speakers. I think he is the best talker of any driver I have ever seen.

Not only that, but he follows this up with his driving skills. Within six months of hearing him on that stage, he went on to win the Indy 500 for the first time.

What else would a team or a manufacturer want from a driver?

He is fast, he has a good work ethic, he communicates well which keeps the sponsors happy and he is an American racing driver in an American championship. He possesses the ultimate mix.

This is the kind of driver the people at the top of our industry are looking for.

The political advantage

You may have noticed that I put "Any political advantages" in my shortlist for what scouts look for. I included this because we get quite a few instances where a driver may be offered an opportunity just because they are politically aligned with a team or manufacturer.

For example, if a driver is fairly good on track but on top of that they happen to be from the same country as the team's sponsors, or they are from a country where the manufacturer wants to sell more products, this can help a driver get through the door.

To give you a specific example, if a race team is run by a company that manufacturers cars, and they want to sell more cars to America, they will be motivated to look for a fast American driver to join their race team.

Always remember motorsport is a business, and tactics like this really do work for manufacturers and sponsors.

This can even be the same for gender. If a company that sponsors a team is interested in helping female drivers because it aligns with their brand, then for marketing reasons they may prefer to employ a female driver to join their race team.

This isn't being sexist or biased towards certain countries due to the sponsor's personal views; it is simply them choosing drivers who fulfil an ambassador role that will help them increase sales away from the track. Again, it's business.

There are at least five drivers that I can name on the current Formula 1 grid who are not there due to their speed, but for political reasons. They are still pretty quick, but their political advantage is what helped the team decide upon them over other (quicker) drivers.

There are many ways in which drivers can use the political card to assist them with opening up career doors, so maybe this is something you can explore with your driver.

On the subject of politics, I would personally resist the temptation to actually pay to be part of a young driver programme.

Between you and me, for obvious reasons the drivers who pay to be on driver programmes hardly ever make it to the top of the sport. They pay obscene amounts of money to wear the F1-branded race suit and race the car in the Formula 1 team's colours, but it's more of a fake social status badge to show others they are going places rather than genuine backing from a Formula 1 team.

There is a lot of this type of bravado in motorsport. Formula 1 teams will happily take money from parents and let you pretend to be one of their young drivers because it's an extra income stream for them. They will then just spend that money on helping the young drivers they actually believe in.

So I wouldn't go down that path if I were you. It's kind of like having a bumper sticker that says "My child goes to Harvard" when in fact they just work there as a window cleaner.

You could pay to be part of a young driver programme if you think it will pull in more sponsors from those who don't understand how the industry works, but just make sure that it will actually work.

You don't want to do this for a year and then leave due to it not working, because that looks like your driver has been dropped from the programme.

I prefer to not play that game.

Help your driver

You obviously don't want to just sit back and hope your driver will be spotted due to their on-track and off-track performances alone. So feel free to contact people of influence so you can put your driver on the radar that way too.

However, your driver must be performing well and getting good results once you have attracted attention to them.

In other words, get your driver to a good level before approaching people. You need to get the 'product' right before you go to market.

With this in mind, I suggest you should look at the three areas that scouts look for, and design a training plan for your driver that helps them improve each area.

There is plenty of advice in this book that will help you do this but if you have people helping you on the performance aspects, get them all aligned with what you want to do. Explain to them the main areas you want to be improved and get them to come up with an action plan for helping your driver.

Your driver will have a 'sell by date' on their head. They will need to prove themselves to those who matter by a certain age, so get clear on what that age is (depending on their long term goal) and create a plan around these time restrictions.

Have a think about how to position your driver politically too. This can mean many things, but you want people to consider your driver on more aspects than just their ability on track. Always ask yourself what else can your driver bring to the party that will suit people of influence in the sport.

All in all, your driver will get spotted if they have earned the right to do so. Couple this with you or your manager knocking on doors, and something will happen.

CHAPTER 21
IT'S A WRAP!

As you are reading this part, I want to commend you for your commitment to becoming the best parent you can be.

This book has been my way of communicating the most important things to remember when helping drivers succeed. There will be many other challenges that you will face as you both tackle the racing world, but if you recycle and modify the advice given here, you will come up with some effective solutions to help you on your way.

Keep coming back to this book to revisit the chapters that are relevant to you at various points of your racing journey, as some may not be applicable today but they may be at a later date. The advice in this book is evergreen so it will be as relevant today as it is in the future. That's because it focuses on the human aspects of our sport: the things we can control.

When it comes to assisting your driver, the main focus should be on helping them learn the personal skills that will help them thrive as an individual. These are the mental skills that will help them in daily life, like to deal with adversity, to create and hunt down a meaningful goal, to learn from their mistakes and for them to fully understand how things work in their industry.

If you can use this sport to teach them these things, they will be just fine – no matter what they end up doing in life.

Main takeaways

As I look back over the chapters of this book, the main things I want you to remember are for you to be certain that racing is something that your child really wants to do. I mean that in their mind, they can't live or breathe without it.

This will fuel them when times get tough – because they will. And on top of that, if their heart and passion is in something else away from racing, we mustn't steal their time from pursuing whatever that other thing is.

They are only young once so if they are passionate about something else, and it is a genuine passion, we need to help them walk that path.

If, however, you are certain that racing is everything to them, compartmentalise things so you can help them improve their driving and their personal skills separately. Get a training plan in place that forces them to improve each and every week, and following each race event.

If you help them structure all of this properly, who knows how far they can go?

Another thing I want to highlight is that you are there to assist your driver... but please resist doing too much for them. We need to teach our young ones the importance of work ethic and discipline.

They must be encouraged to run the show and be the leader in their own career. This will be driven by their desire to succeed, but they must possess the personal skills to steer their ship themselves.

If all of this is done correctly, you will both be on a wild ride together and you can proudly watch them create the life they want. What a privileged position you are in!

I wish you and your child all the best – and please do contact me to share your experiences.

Thank you so much for reading this book and feel free to reach out if there is anything I can do to help.

Enzo

Printed in Great Britain
by Amazon

26530774R00159